Advance Praise for *Quote 3*

"Nobody lives long enough to make all their own mistakes. That's why we must learn from others", to paraphrase Sam Levenson. *Quote 3* by Michael Weaver is one of those books that gives us lessons from losses that help us win bigger and faster.

Quote 3 is full of life lessons that will magnify your results. Realizing that "How you do one thing is how you do everything" alone will change the way you think, work, and lead. Michael reveals the critical value of discipline and routines to sustainable success. He explains how working with the right people is the right way to build a business and that it is not just good enough to reach out to prospects, you must talk with them.

And his 12-Second Approach idea can change your results for the better forever. He provides relationship building and questioning tactics that will help you be more referrable and grow your business, whatever you do. You'll discover the little-known secret to successful closing, that escapes so many sales professionals and I assure you he is bang on! Truly, the very premise of the book, *Quote 3* alone is a simple game changer.

Finally, Michael wraps up the book by showing you how to apply his experience to your teams, so you don't just talk about success, you make it happen. You can be the best when you learn from the experience of those who've been there, like Michael Weaver."

— Jim F ⸻ ⸻ft Media Group

HOW TO MAKE
MULTIPLE 6 FIGURES
IN ANY SALES ORGANIZATION

QUOTE 3

MICHAEL WEAVER

SAVIO
REPVBLIC

A SAVIO REPUBLIC BOOK
An Imprint of Post Hill Press
ISBN: 979-8-88845-592-0
ISBN (eBook): 979-8-88845-593-7

Quote 3:
How to Make Multiple 6 Figures in Any Sales Organization
© 2024 by Michael Weaver
All Rights Reserved

Cover Design by Cody Corcoran

This is a work of nonfiction. All people, locations, events, and situations are portrayed to the best of the author's memory.

posthillpress.com
New York • Nashville
Published in the United States of America

1 2 3 4 5 6 7 8 9 10

To my wife, Courtney, thank you for your unwavering support and for always being in my corner on both the good days and the hard days. I love you!

CONTENTS

INTRODUCTION

YOU ARE IN SALES. You work hard, day in and day out, to hit your targets, to reach your quota, to make your numbers. You know it's a grind. You know it's hard. But you're fine with that. You knew the game when you got into sales, so challenge accepted. But those targets are becoming harder and harder to hit. And grinding it out, putting in that extra time—those extra hours and days each month—doesn't seem to be paying off like it used to. Is it you? Have you lost your touch? Have you forgotten how to close? Self-doubt creeps in.

But it shouldn't. Because if you're like most people in sales, you were sold a giant lie when you first got into the game. Yep, you heard me right—lied to. We all were.

So what's the lie?

"Just do more!"

Make *more* calls. Take *more* appointments. Do *more* quotes. Buy *more* leads. Hire *more* people. And of course, my favorite:

work *more* hours. Just do *more,* and *more,* and *more*…and then after that, when you think you've done all you can, do some *more.*

Sound familiar?

This is exactly what I was taught. My career in sales started when I was twenty-one years old. I was a junior in college, still didn't know for sure what I wanted to do in life, and was leaning towards going to law school. I needed an internship prior to my senior year so I could graduate when I completed my upcoming senior year. So instead of going to Panama City Beach for Spring Break to party my ass off, I decided to do the responsible thing and look for an internship for the upcoming summer.

I went around and applied at multiple law offices, as well as a bunch of banks. All of them felt literally like funeral homes when I walked into them, and I was dreading the upcoming summer. Good news for me—none of them were interested anyways. So then I started applying at insurance agencies. Again, they all felt like funeral homes—until I stumbled into a young, energetic insurance agency.

The office had a cool, high-energy vibe. I was thinking to myself, "This is what I'm talking about!" Even though it was insurance, at least the office environment could be fun. So I applied, interviewed, and was told to come back upon graduating, which would've been great except for the small fact that I had to have an internship prior to graduating. I decided I would go back the next day and try to convince the owner to hire me.

I showed up before anyone else. As I was sitting in the parking lot, I saw a silver Lexus pull up and park. As the owner of the company got out of the car, he looked over his shoulder, and we made eye contact. I thought to myself, "Well, here goes nothing." So I got out of the car as he unlocked the office and walked in. I followed not too far behind. He greeted me in somewhat of a confused manner, which makes sense because, well, I didn't belong there. But he didn't kick me out, so I told him I planned on showing up daily until he gives me a job.

Reflecting back on it all, it sounds pretty insane. But sometimes crazy is what's required, because he agreed to give me a shot. He gave me an opportunity a few days a week as their marketing intern, which really meant I was a combination of a cold calling expert and the office janitor. I was responsible for lead generation and doing everything in the office that no one else wanted to do.

By the time the summer was over, he offered me a full-time position when I graduated, which would be May of 2010. And boom! Just like that, I had a job coming straight out of college. This was also the birth of my sales career.

Fast forward to April of 2014. I am now about to start my own business as a "scratch" insurance agency owner. Scratch just means that I didn't have any clients or a book of business when I started—in other words, I was starting from ground zero. Actually my wife, Courtney, and I started this business together. This was incredibly exciting for us, but it also meant we only had $5,000 to our name and now no source of guaranteed income between us. We put ourselves in a do-or-die situation—literally. We had no other plan other than to make this work. And if we didn't make this work, we would end up with nothing. We burned the boats with no backup plan, baby!

How did we come to make such a risky decision? Over the previous three years selling insurance products, I was the highest producing insurance sales person in the Kansas City area. I was ready for the next step and convinced Courtney this was the right move. I had planned on running the business similar to how I was taught at the insurance firm. Work a lot of hours, make 150 to 300 calls a day, quote as many new prospects as possible, train the team to do the same, and it will all work out. The plan was foolproof... until it all kind of fell apart.

It started out okay. I hustled and got a lead company to give me fifty thousand leads to call. We were in business! The team and I got to work. Each person on the team was expected to make a minimum of 150 calls a day. My Territory Sales Manager at the time agreed this should be enough activity but that we may have to do more (there's that word again) if it doesn't get us the results we were aiming for.

I was pushing my team hard. But that's all I was doing—pushing. I wasn't helping them. I wasn't teaching them. My coaching skills at the time were terrible. I would just say what I was taught. I would spew the big lie: make *more* calls and work *more* hours if you need to. Just do *more* and do whatever it takes. Whatever you do, you have to hit your numbers.

You know what happens, when you just keep telling people to do more and more and more—and they listen? They burn out. Seven months in I lost my first employee. He was toast. He was tired of making over 150 calls every single day. He said it wasn't fun and he wasn't enjoying what he did. He got into the business to change people's lives and felt like that was an impossible task doing what I was asking him to do. Not only was he burnt out, he was unfulfilled.

You would have thought I learned my lesson after this first incident, but nope! I was young and arrogant and, in hindsight, entirely ignorant of what I needed to do to be successful, to create a prosperous business. So instead of reflecting on my own failings as a leader or looking for flaws in the business model I had created, I blamed this one employee for not being smart enough or resilient enough or dedicated enough to do what needed to be done— which of course was simply *more*. Nope, instead of changing a thing, I just continued to run this same Model of More for the first eighteen months of my young business owner career.

Then the unthinkable happened. I burnt out myself! I was working over fifteen-hour days, every day. I was cycling through team members. They came and went. I worked them until they couldn't work anymore, and then I just got someone else in to take their place. But it was all so soulless. The same model of more, over and over again, with no regard for the people I had working for me or even what it was that we were selling. Through it all, I lost my passion for insurance and sales altogether.

This isn't to say it was all a complete failure. To the outside world and my industry more broadly, everything looked good. The numbers looked solid. To the industry at large, we looked like we were on solid footing. We looked like rock stars actually! We were one of the top one hundred agencies in the country out of over twenty thousand agencies. However, I was miserable. I had to take some time to really think about things. I had to reevaluate what I wanted, what I wanted from my business, who I was as a person—all of it—because I knew one thing for certain: Things had to change. And when I say things had to change, I mean everything.

I decided I was going to do a complete 180 from the Model of More I had been running. Rather than go for sheer quantity, I was going to strive for quality instead. Moving forward, we would take a quality first approach in all facets of the business. This meant quality team members, quality conversations, quality clients, and a quality life.

I started coaching the team to not focus on so many calls, but to focus on the conversations they were having with those who did answer the phone. We created an "ideal customer" avatar and focused on working with those types of customers. We began focusing on turning customers into raving fans by building and establishing relationships with them. We began to focus on a transformational interaction from start to finish versus a transactional interaction, which is all we previously did with our high-volume model of more.

And as we changed our entire approach, everything actually did begin to change—for the better. My team and I began beating and then crushing expectations. We were helping more people and making more money than ever before. We went from top one hundred to number thirty-two. Even better, I was working *less* (not *more*) than ever! I was happy. I had found my passion again and was loving life.

With our new model and newfound success, we decided to open a few more businesses and duplicate the sales blueprint we had created by implementing it in new and different sales industries. Courtney started an online fitness business and sold over $100,000 in services within six months of the launch. She then started a direct sales company selling skin care products. Within two years, she was ranked fourteen out of forty-three thousand! Then we started an SEO company and, like the fitness business, we made over $100,000 in less than six months.

It was working. All of it. Not only had we been successful selling in different sales industries, but we opened a coaching business to coach insurance sales producers. We taught them the same strategies we were using so successfully, and they started seeing an increase in their sales and revenue as well.

These same strategies and techniques we have implemented to build multiple six and seven figure businesses, and the same strategies and techniques we have taught to over ten thousand sales professionals on their roads to success are going to be exactly what we teach you about in this book with our proven Quote 3 method!

Mind you, this is going to go against everything you've been taught. We are, first and foremost, tossing out the big lie of "more." Even if you don't read any further, please understand and take away this very basic truth: *More* and *more* and *more* of the wrong thing merely leads to *more* wrong things—and the wrong things never lead to the right things. It's that simple. But it's one thing to know what *not* to do, it's another to know what *to* do. And if you are willing to listen, I am willing to help!

It doesn't matter if you sell tangible or intangible products, if you want to be successful in sales, this book is for you. It doesn't matter if you sell insurance, cars, financial planning, private jets, or coaching services. Maybe you are in direct sales, yes, this is for you. If you own a business, definitely for you. If you manage a sales team, yep, this is for you. This book is going to teach you exactly how to be successful—and just as importantly, it's going to teach you how to achieve success by doing *less*, not more! In fact, doing less actually leads to more—more sales, more money, more referrals, more confidence, and more fulfillment!

Not only will you learn our Quote 3 method but you will also learn everything in between, from marketing to the sales conversation, to creating your ideal customer and turning them into devout fans! After reading this book, you will feel more confident than ever and be prepared to not only hit your sales goals every month, but be ready to crush them!

Are you ready to begin changing your sales career, your business, and your life? Then let's get started!

1

EMBRACING CHANGE

CHARLIE WAS A SUCCESSFUL business owner. He owned an insurance agency and was in the top 3 percent of the company he represented. Charlie first approached me because he was a year into his second agency and both him and that business were struggling. His original office also began to have issues.

I'll never forget what Charlie told me on our first call when I was going through our initial discovery conversation. "Michael," he said, "I feel like I've tried everything, but nothing is working. I'm about to just call it quits and shut the second location down."

You see, Charlie was frustrated. He was overwhelmed, he was upset, he was feeling like a failure. His business had high turnover. He couldn't keep his employees in the door. He was working more than he had in years, and the worst part was that he was making less money than he was with just one agency.

I wish I couldn't relate, but it reminded me of my past all over again, when I was ready to hang it up and was questioning whether insurance sales and agency ownership were for me. That was exactly what I shared with Charlie. I let him know he wasn't alone. I had been there and so had thousands of others. Wanting to quit and give up on your dreams is never an easy feeling to work through. It can be depressing and lonely, and I wouldn't wish that feeling on anyone.

"Let's push the pause button on you shutting down your second business," I said. "Let's dig a little more into your business model and your approach to sales."

His answers were all similar. They all revolved around the Big Lie—the Model of More. He was spending *more* money on marketing. He was buying *more* leads. He was pushing his team to make *more* calls. He was hiring more sales producers. He was telling his team to do a minimum of ten quotes a day per person. He was working *more* hours and encouraging his team to do the same. Just do *more*! That was his plan. His only plan. And it wasn't working.

Sound familiar?

The problem with *more* in Charlie's case, my case, and very likely your case, too, is that more leads to more stress, more anxiety, and more feeling overwhelmed, but ultimately less money, less success, and less happiness. It also leads to more turnover and less production in the business.

When I talked to some of his sales producers, they felt similar. They had no confidence and high anxiety; they weren't reaching goals. They felt like they were letting both themselves and Charlie down. I remember one producer even saying, "We come in, we do more than we are asked, *and* we still can't hit the goals. It sucks."

Can you relate?

The thing was, Charlie felt like the team was doing all the activities it took to be successful or at least what they had been taught to do to be successful in sales—yet the exact opposite was happening. Everyone was doing more and accomplishing less.

When you run into a wall like this, it's incredibly frustrating and disheartening. You have an overwhelming feeling of wanting to give up and throw in the towel. You feel like a failure, letting your employees down, your family down, yourself down.

So I asked Charlie a simple question, "Would you be willing to try something new, a totally new methodology for ninety days?"

He agreed. "I'm out of options," he said. "I'll try anything to make it work because what I'm doing now just isn't cutting it."

I could hear the desperation in his voice. In fact, I've heard it in a lot of people's voices. In a way, that's a good thing. Because I know that person is passionate. I know that person cares deeply about what they do, and they care deeply about succeeding. As someone in sales, you know that this is the kind of passion and commitment you need to succeed—but it's not the only thing. You also need the right approach. You need the right skills to truly succeed and come out on top of the competition.

So if you can relate to Charlie or Charlie's team, I ask you the same question. Are you willing to try something new? Something that goes against what you have been taught your entire sales career? Could you reset everything you know and completely commit to my method for ninety days?

If you answered, yes, congratulations! You took a crucial first step to success. The first step to change is simply being willing to change. And that's no small decision. Change is scary. Change is hard. To accept change means being willing to be scared, anxious, put out of your comfort zone. Being willing to change is also humbling because you have to admit you don't have all the answers—that as much as you do know, you don't know it all.

But as scary and as humbling as it is, accepting change is also incredibly brave. Why? Because it's scary and humbling! It takes a brave and honest person to try something new, to put themselves out there and push past the fear of the unknown. This is the first step to changing your sales career and your life—forever.

I still remember the feeling I had in 2016 when I felt like I was at my breaking point and ready to throw in the towel on my dreams of running a successful business and insurance agency. I went through a state of depression and felt like an absolute and total failure. The hardest part, I felt like I had to hide it from everyone. My team, my peers, my parents and, yes, even my wife. I didn't want to look weak. I didn't want to look like I didn't have my shit together. To the outside world, I was wildly successful, crushing business as a twenty-eight-year-old. I looked as if I was living the American dream. On the inside though, I was crumbling and felt like a fraud. Sure the "success" was there, we were top of the production charts and making good money, but I was *miserable*.

Even though I didn't verbally tell Courtney what was going on and was trying to hide it from her, she knew something was up and confronted me about eight weeks into it. You see, not only is Courtney my wife and business partner, she is my biggest cheerleader and supporter. She could see right through me and what was going on and was trying to let me go through the process of it all but eventually decided to step in and have a conversation. In all fairness, I was more edgy than usual and would snap at her for the littlest of things. It wasn't fair to her at all, and she was incredibly patient with me—but one day she decided enough was enough.

She approached me and said, "What's going on? Something is off and has been off with you for a couple of months." I tried to play it off, but she cornered me and said, "It's okay, just tell me what's going on."

And it was then that I just lost it. I broke down and started crying because I couldn't find the words. Not only could I not find the words at that time, but I had been holding in all of these emotions for months and I couldn't handle it anymore. Finally after a few minutes, I was able to gather myself and tell her what was going on. I told her that I was feeling like a failure, that I was unhappy, that I didn't even want to go into the office most days, that I felt like I was in my own personal prison. I told her I was ready to quit and throw in the towel with the business and try to find something else to do with my life. I told her I didn't know what I wanted to do yet, but I would figure it out and we would be okay. It was at this moment that she recommended we sit down and talk through the situation and what had happened to get me to this point. That was exactly what we did.

Through this self-reflection, I discovered I was burnt out and that things had to change. Doing *more* of what I was doing was a recipe for disaster and unhappiness no matter how much money I made. It was at this point I realized I had to start doing things that lit me up and that I found meaningful. Not only this, but I had to change the way I was leading my team and organization and the way we were treating customers. How could I create a transformational experience for everyone involved, including myself? What did I really want for my future and the future of my business? How could I wake up every day on fire and enjoy what I did and have a team around me that enjoyed what they did?

I had to take the time to figure all of these things out. So now it's your turn. Let's start doing some self-reflection. Right now, how do you currently feel in your day-to-day sales career?

- Frustrated
- Excited
- Overwhelmed
- Happy
- Anxious
- Confident
- Depressed
- Confused
- Something else

Really take some time to think about how you feel on a daily basis and write these feelings down.

Now I want you to write down your feelings about change. How does the prospect of change make you feel?

- Excited
- Nervous
- Anxious
- Scared
- Confused
- Something else

Lastly, I want you to write down how you want to feel daily. How would you want to feel day to day?

- Confident
- Successful
- Purposeful
- Excited

- Fulfilled
- Happy

Save your answers now because they are going to serve as benchmarks of your journey to success. When we've completed your journey, you will be able to look back to how you felt before we began. Then you can gauge how you think about change after going through the process in comparison to how you felt about it now, before you actually started it. And then finally, you can answer the final question to evaluate where you are, and then continue to evaluate the progress you're making in trying to achieve how you want to feel on a daily basis.

So now that you've taken this big first step, now that you've committed to change, you are ready for step two! Let's go!

2

HOW YOU DO ONE THING IS HOW YOU DO EVERYTHING

IN 2018, I EMBARKED on a fitness competition journey. I had six months to not only get in shape but also be ready to step on stage to show the world just how fit I was (or was not). Obviously, there was no way I was going to stand on stage in front of over a thousand spectators to be judged and not give it my all.

The first step was hiring a coach. This, to me, was a change in and of itself. I had never had a workout or fitness "coach" in my life. But I realized that if I wanted to get into the shape I truly wanted, I couldn't do it all on my own. I simply didn't know enough about maximizing my workouts. I didn't know enough about diet and nutrition. In short, I didn't have all the answers. I had to accept that fact in order to move forward and make a positive change in my life.

Of course, there was some trial and error. Not all fitness coaches are created equal, and there's also the "goodness of fit" issue—meaning I also had to find a fitness coach who was not only knowledgeable and expressed a high degree of expertise, but also knew how to motivate and engage who I was as a person. I finally decided on one coach who checked all the boxes, and it turned out to be a game changer. My coach completely elevated my workouts, my mindset, my diet—everything I needed to reach my goals.

This brings us to the second step, which was increasing my commitment and discipline. My coach wanted me working out six days a week. That kind of commitment was easy when I was a teenager, but it was an entirely different ask as an adult with a wife and multiple businesses. But if I wanted to not make a fool of myself on stage, I knew I had to follow this plan. I knew I had to fully commit. And I did.

The third and most difficult step for me was being disciplined with my diet. I had to not only eat healthier, but I also had to eat completely differently than I was used to. I was suddenly having to eat five meals a day, seven days a week, which equates to thirty-five meals a week. Thirty-five meals a week multiplied by four weeks is 140 meals a month. And out of those 140 meals, *only four* of those could be cheat meals. The most difficult part of the meals was that the food was extremely bland and that the magical brown water I enjoy on occasion (bourbon) was off limits.

I'm not lying; after a few days of eating like that, I had a big WTF moment, as in WTF did I get into? Eating 136 meals a month of nothing but eggs, chicken, rice, and broccoli is what! On top of that, in terms of alcohol consumption, I was limited to one four-ounce glass of red wine on Saturdays. To say that I looked forward to every Saturday night where I sat down, enjoyed a few slices of pizza and a nice glass of red wine is an understatement. That pizza and red wine is honestly what got me through most weeks. It was a way to reward myself for being disciplined throughout the week.

So for six long (very long) months, I hit the gym daily, six days a week like clockwork. I met with my coach weekly for check-ins. I ate the right foods, at the right time, and avoided the bad ones all of the time, aside from my small moments where I could cheat on Saturday nights. For six freaking months, I stayed disciplined to the process.

Did I want to quit? Absolutely!

Did I want to cheat? Yes!

Did I question my sanity and why I was even competing in this stupid competition? One hundred percent!

Six months came and went, and it was showtime. After six grueling months of insanely hard work and sacrifice, it was time to compete. It was time to step on stage. In my very first National Physique Competition, I placed and medaled in both categories I competed in! Sure, maybe I didn't win first place, but I medaled. More importantly, I proved to myself that I could be disciplined and accomplish whatever I want in life if it was important to me. Even more importantly, I put myself out there. I stepped on a stage in nothing but swimming trunks and was judged for how I looked and the work I had put in.

It's truly amazing what a person can accomplish when they have a goal and are hyper-focused and intentional with their actions for an extended period of time. I proved to myself that hard work, sacrifice, and intentional focus partnered with time is the recipe for success and hitting goals.

You may be asking yourself what any of this has to do with sales. Well, it has everything to do with sales. In fact, it has every-thing to do with life.

You see, how you do one thing is how you do everything. You're either all in or you're not. You're either disciplined or you're not. The best part is, you have the choice to be who you are and who you are not. Yes, *you* get to decide. It doesn't matter what has happened in the past. That's in the rearview mirror and you need to be focused on what is in front of you, what you want, and who you need to become to get there.

But I completely know putting things in the past can be hard. I know forgetting about bad things that have happened or things that didn't go your way or things that you made mistakes on or could've done better can be really tough to do. If you're like me, you probably hear one criticism far more loudly than all the praise. That's part of being a perfectionist. You want everything to be right, to work right, always. But that's not possible, and, more importantly, we can't change what's behind us, we can't change what's already happened. All we can do is move forward and do it better the next time.

I like to think about it in terms of sports. All of the great ath-letes have "amnesia." It doesn't matter how well they played in a game, or how badly they played. Once it's done, it's done, and they move on. If Patrick Mahomes throws an interception, he doesn't sit there and dwell on it. He doesn't start handing the ball off every play. He goes back out there and slings the pigskin on the very next play. If Aaron Judge strikes out in his first at-bat, he doesn't stand there with the bat on his shoulder for the rest of the game. He steps up to the plate and takes his cuts just the way he always does. If LeBron James has an off shooting night, he doesn't just pass the ball for the rest of the season. He steps onto the court the next game and shoots himself back into sync. The best players, the greatest players, put mistakes behind them as quickly as they made them. They learn from their mistakes; they don't live in them. If they did, they would never achieve greatness. In fact, they would never achieve anything.

And so that's the approach you have to take now. No doubt you've learned some lessons from your experiences—both good and bad. But now you need to put the past in the past so that you can completely embrace the change you need to live in the present and move forward.

The purpose of this chapter is to help you set yourself up for success because success just doesn't happen by accident. To be able to accomplish what we discuss in the following chapters, you are going to have to build your discipline and confidence muscles. Confidence is created by disciplined action for a sustained amount of time. Let's face it, sales is the most difficult career and profession in the world. It's not always going to be rainbows and sunshine. There are days you are going to want to quit. There will be days you don't want to put in the work. Guess what though? To reap the rewards that sales careers have to offer, you have to show up! You have to be present. You have to be willing to do what others aren't. If you are going to be in the top 1 percent of producers and income earners in the world, you have to be willing to do what the other 99 percent aren't willing to do. That starts with being disciplined and showing up.

Discipline Starts with Routines

The easiest way to build your discipline and confidence muscles is to have a consistent daily routine. I will take it a step further and say a consistent morning routine. I am not going to say that to be successful you have to have a morning routine, because there are individuals out there who are wildly successful and openly talk about sleeping in, that don't believe in morning routines. And that's great for them. There are exceptions to every single rule in the book. I will say, however, that a majority of highly successful individuals I know who make six, seven, and even eight figures, have a successful morning routine that they stick to daily. Yes, I am talking about the 5:00 a.m. club. There is something about getting up before the sun, getting your body moving, focusing on your physical and mental health that I truly believe is a competitive advantage in both your career and your life.

Just as "how you do one thing is how you do everything," "how you start your day sets the standard for how you live your day." If you start your day not really caring if you get out of bed or not at a certain time, then that kind of attitude can very well seep into the rest of your day in subtle ways. Maybe you don't care quite as much about meeting that last prospective client or making that last call. If you don't feel like you need to be the first one up in the morning, then maybe you don't feel that you need to be first in anything, that it's okay to be second or third or tenth.

Don't get me wrong, I don't want to overstate this. It's not as if sleeping in once in a while means the death of your career in sales or that pushing the snooze button sometimes means you're a slacker who doesn't care about anything. What I'm saying is that if you start the day in attack mode, if you are pushing yourself every day in the same way to get out of bed, to start your day, then you're more likely to live the rest of your day in that same manner, with that same mindset—aggressively attacking the day, acting upon the world rather than the world acting upon you. You can't establish that mindset in a day. You can't just say to yourself "tomorrow I'm going to get up at the crack of dawn and really jumpstart my day," and have that be enough. That changes only that day, not your whole life. You can't even just make up your mind to do that for a whole week and think that's going to change anything. You have to, as I said earlier, fully commit. You have to be all in. That starts with a morning routine that doesn't allow you to question what you do or do not do or when you will or will not get up. The routine you create sets those rules, and then you have to live by them. That's how you start building discipline.

I truly believe that my morning routine is why I am who I am today and why in less than a decade I have been able to accomplish what I have accomplished, both personally and professionally. It has been a game changer in my life. Every successful person I have surrounded myself with also has a morning routine. If you can be disciplined with a routine, get out of bed when it's dark outside even though you want to hit the snooze button and stay in bed, you can be disciplined with anything and everything in life, including your career and the activities you need to be doing daily. Discipline creates confidence though small daily wins, every single day. Getting out of bed and accomplishing your morning routine daily, means you are winning daily. That means you are growing your confidence muscle every single day. Simply put, you are creating a better version of yourself daily that is going to carry over into your career.

So I am going to share my morning routine and what works well for me to give you an idea of what I am talking about. I am also going to share ideas from other people I admire and respect that are slightly different from my routine but also really helpful.

Make Your Routine Enjoyable

Making your routine enjoyable is the first and perhaps the most important tip for establishing a routine that you will actually stick to. If you create a routine that is a grind from the start, that you dread doing as you go to sleep at night, then it will never work. It won't last. Eventually the grind will overtake your willingness to do it, and, slowly but surely, you'll end up with no routine at all. So you need to create a routine that you look forward to every day—something that is going to help you grow, physically, mentally, emotionally, and spiritually.

Here's what my perfect morning routine currently looks like:

5:02 a.m. – Wake up

5:15 a.m. – Start twelve-minute High Intensity Interval Training (HIIT) workout in home gym

5:30 a.m. – Get in sauna for breathing exercise, meditation, and prayer

6:00 a.m. – Sauna session ends, and I begin reading

6:30 a.m. – Journal

6:45 a.m. – Check phone

7:00 a.m. – Go on walk with Courtney and the dogs

This is my perfect morning routine and something I am very disciplined with. It's perfect for me because it hits all four aspects that are needed to fully engage and embrace the day—that is, it addresses the physical, mental, emotional, and spiritual aspects of myself that are vital to feel whole, healthy, and energized.

So you'll notice that I've tailored my routine with some quirks. Like, I start at 5:02 rather than 5:00 a.m. sharp. Is that weird? Yep! But you know what? It works for me, and that's the only thing that matters when you're creating your routine—what works for you.

So when I started my routine, my goal, obviously, was to start at 5:00 a.m. But there was something about it that, psychologically, was bothering me. In my head, anything in the 4:00 a.m. range seemed SO early, and 5:00 a.m. was just one minute after the 4:00 a.m. range! As crazy as it sounds, I decided to give myself those two extra minutes—two extra minutes that would put me more fully in the 5 o'clock hour. And you know what? It worked! That one little quirk made it easier for me to wake up. I didn't dread it any longer, and that's all that mattered. So for the past ten years, that's when I wake up: 5:02 a.m.

You'll also notice that I don't really do anything until 5:15. That's because I'm not a robot. I don't just hear the alarm and pop right up. I allow myself a few minutes to wake up. I don't treat my alarm like a military Reveille on a bugle. My alarm goes off and I give myself a few minutes to wake up, get oriented, and then start my day.

The first thing I do is my twelve-minute HIIT workout. Yes, it's a jolt for sure—but that's why I do it. It packs a great workout into a short span of time, so, to me, it's the ideal. It gets my body moving, my blood flowing, my muscles pumping. It gets me physically ready to engage the day.

My sauna session checks multiple boxes. First, it's beneficial physically, sweating out toxins and impurities. Plus, it's a great wind-down from the HIIT workout. It also checks the emotional and spiritual boxes. I practice box breathing during my sauna session which leads into a meditation. I breathe in for five seconds, hold my breath for five seconds, breathe out slowly for five seconds, hold for five seconds, and then repeat that for approximately twenty to twenty-five minutes. It makes me feel at one with my thoughts. I then will take the last five to ten minutes to go through my prayer exercise. It's calming and allows me time to reflect.

There is just something about getting out of a sauna and being covered in sweat looking like you just got out of a swimming pool. It's a feeling that is hard to explain, but it's fulfilling and addicting.

The half-hour I spend reading checks the mental box. I start each day feeding myself intellectually with different thoughts, perspectives, and ideas. Sometimes it's about sales specifically, other times it's about business more broadly, and still other times it's about life in general—different approaches to living, philosophies about life, and ways of thinking. Basically, I read anything that I find interesting and that will get me thinking and stimulate my mind.

The journaling I do checks multiple boxes as well—mental, emotional, spiritual. It's a way to help me synthesize my thoughts. I don't put limits on what I can or cannot journal about. I use it to help me think through whatever's going on in my life at the time. Sometimes that might be more personal in nature—things I'm experiencing with Courtney or my family or maybe even just feelings I'm experiencing myself. Other times, it's about different things going on with our businesses—new ideas we might try to increase revenue in one business or another, or maybe new business ideas altogether. Or sometimes it's as immediate as journaling about what I've just read. I might just take the time to process that morning's reading. Ultimately, I find this time dedicated to journaling to be a type of meditation in itself and a way to get my thoughts down on paper.

After that, I start to ease into the business of the day. I take fifteen minutes to check my phone. This just allows me to get a heads up on what will be on the day's agenda, such as making sure there are no immediate fires that will need attending to.

After that, I go on a walk with Courtney and the dogs. This allows me to make sure I start each day connecting with Courtney.

The walking obviously again promotes my physical well-being, but more importantly I'm prioritizing the relationship that matters most in my life. Courtney and I are partners in everything, so it's important that we start each day spending quality time together.

By 7:30 a.m., I feel complete. I feel happy, satisfied. Having nourished myself physically, mentally, emotionally, and spiritually, I feel as though I'm already winning the day.

But I want to be clear about one thing: this all sounds great, and it is, but, as I said, I'm not a robot. I am far from perfect. So many talking heads in today's culture almost shame you if you aren't perfect, like they never have bad days. That's of course bullshit. There are days where I sleep in. There are days where I hit the snooze button. There are days when, yes, it's a grind, and days when it doesn't happen at all. No one, and I mean *no one*, is perfect and everyone has cheat days. If not, I would go insane. We all would.

That said, most days—and I mean 99 percent of days—I show up. I show up for myself. I show up for my wife. I show up for my family. I show up for my future self. Ultimately, we all lose some battles. But when you repeatedly show up, you will definitely win the war.

So your routine will look different than mine for sure. That's a good thing. You need to do what's best for you. What's going to allow you to hit those four crucial aspects of physical, mental, emotional, and spiritual health?

Move your body! Maybe you do a HIIT workout, maybe you do yoga, maybe you go on a run or walk, maybe you hit the gym, maybe it's Pilates. It doesn't matter. Whatever gets you moving and working your muscles is what you should do to ensure you're optimizing your physical health.

As for the emotional and spiritual side, maybe it's meditation, maybe it's prayer, maybe it's breathing exercises, maybe it's reading from a religious text—whatever allows you to feel nourished in these ways is what you need to make part of your morning routine.

For the mental aspect, read or do some kind of personal development daily. Read, podcast, Audible—whatever will allow you intellectual inputs to stimulate your thoughts and curiosity about the world around you.

And last, but definitely not least, be intentional in making time for those relationships more personal and closer to you. Make time, quality time, for your partner and family each day. In my experience, when the most important relationships in your life are good, everything else seems to go good as well.

In addition to creating a routine you enjoy, make sure you're not afraid to change it up as well. In addition to being enjoyable, your routine should also challenge you. Part of keeping things both enjoyable and challenging is to change the routine now and again. I tend to change my routine every nine to twelve months to some degree. I still hit the four major aspects of physical, mental, emotional, and spiritual health, but I switch things up to keep myself interested and engaged. For example, as I am finishing this chapter, I just started a new morning routine, and I am back to hitting the weights in the gym and I couldn't be more excited. Yes, it's an adjustment and I have had to create a new "perfect" morning routine. Prior to going to the gym, I am getting out of bed and hitting the sauna for my thirty-minute meditation and prayer session. I then journal prior to heading to the gym. Now my reading is done in the truck on the way to the gym and on the way home from the gym. I have incorporated cold water therapy into my routine, and I'm doing plunges right when I get home. Then I go on a walk with Courtney and the dogs.

Your routine needs to be fun and something you look forward to daily. It needs to be energizing! Don't fall into the trap of trying to make your morning routine productive and efficient and just another task to mark off for the day. That defeats the entire purpose of a successful morning routine. Take this simple advice: if you don't make it enjoyable, you won't enjoy it!

A couple of great additional resources for morning routines are the books, *The Miracle Morning* by Hal Elrod and *The 5AM Club* by Robin Sharma. These books do a deep dive into the benefits of morning routines and why you should do them.

Finally, as I mentioned earlier, your routine doesn't have to be a morning routine. While I am a firm believer that when you win your morning, you win your day, there are many successful people who don't believe in a morning routine. They do, however, believe in a success routine. I would agree with them. You don't have to be a morning person to be successful and thrive in life or in your career, *but* you do have to have some kind of success routine because this builds discipline and confidence. Maybe you work out midday to get re-energized or maybe you are a night owl, and your routine is in the evening when your creative juices are flowing. Maybe you break it up over the day and read over a cup of coffee, meditate to end your lunch break, go on a walk after work to trigger the mindset that work is over and now it's personal time, and journal right before you go to bed about the things that you enjoyed about the day or anything else that might be on your mind.

My wife, for example, is one of the most brilliant and successful entrepreneurs and business owners I know, yet her routine is completely different from mine. She doesn't get up until after 6:30 a.m. most days. We then will typically hit the gym together. We will go on a walk with the dogs when we get home from the gym, as I said before. She then starts the rest of her success routine which involves journaling, typically going on a long walk by her-self, or doing yoga. She usually listens to a book on the walk and then meditates when she gets back. She is a night owl and creative juices flow for her in the evenings, so a lot of times she will also journal in the evenings as well.

There is no way Courtney is getting up at 5:00 a.m., yet she is wildly successful! Make your routine yours so that it is something that you look forward to and is fun, yet challenges you mentally and physically.

Your success routine is your competitive advantage in busi-ness and in life!

Exercise

Take the time now to sketch out what a successful routine might look like for you. Make sure that you are following the two main criteria I discussed: making it something you enjoy, and making it so that you will nourish yourself physically, mentally, emotionally, and spiritually.

3

SILVER BULLET SOLUTION

REMEMBER CHARLIE? CHARLIE WAS so frustrated with his team's results (or lack thereof) he was ready to give up on his second office after a year of being open. Who would blame him? He was stressed to the max, overwhelmed with running two offices, frustrated because he felt like he wasn't doing enough to set his team up for success, and, on top of all that, he was making less money than before when he had only one business.

If you also recall, I asked Charlie if he would give it ninety more days. Just not give it ninety more days, but give it everything he had, go all in to implement new strategies and a new way of doing things. I had cautioned him that this would be a strategy that at first may sound crazy because it went against everything he had been taught when it comes to sales. It went against the big lie model of more—more calls, more hours, more pivots, more marketing, more team members, more appointments, more quotes—that simply doing more would bring success.

The problem with this is, there is absolutely zero clarity when it comes to just doing more. More doesn't lead to purpose. More doesn't lead to fulfillment. More doesn't lead to more money, weirdly enough. More is purely a strategy of hope, a hope that you do enough to hit your goals.

So when Charlie agreed to give me his ninety days of full commitment, I introduced him to my winning formula. I introduced him to the Quote 3 method.

The Quote 3 method is actually remarkably straightforward: It's an approach where every single day, you quote/propose your product or service to three new prospects who you don't currently work with. If you have a team, each individual would be responsible for quoting/proposing your product/service to three new prospects a day. It's that simple and exactly why the Quote 3 method works so well.

The name itself—Quote 3—is pretty self-explanatory. You are responsible for quoting or proposing your product or service to three new people every day who you don't currently work with. The simplicity is not only powerful, but it creates a sense of clarity and confidence! You know that every single day this is what you are responsible for. If you manage or run a sales team, then every person on the team is held accountable to getting three quotes or proposals out a day, which makes your job as the sales leader and manager extremely easy. Lastly, this will create buy in. It's simple to understand, the expectation is clear, and it's a powerful message that you and your team can get behind.

The Quote 3 method also creates freedom and flexibility because it's such a manageable target. You're not demanding some astronomical number each day. You're not saying quote twenty, quote fifty. You're not constantly upping the ante and telling yourself and everyone around you to quote *more*. You know that all you have to do, or your team has to do, is quote three new prospects a day, every day, to be successful. Those three quotes a day are what is keeping you from crushing it in sales and making multiple six figures or even more depending on the sales industry you are in! If that isn't good news, I honestly don't know what is.

I came up with the name Quote 3 because in the insurance industry we were always focused on getting "quotes" out to prospects. The name just stuck. It didn't matter if it was insurance, our coaching business, fitness business, direct sales, or SEO, we were always focused on talking to three new prospects a day and getting quotes out. You may say proposal, application, or another term I am unaware of. A quote is a quote, and you just need to Quote 3 new prospects a day to be wildly successful in sales, regardless of the industry.

Now if you are anything like Charlie, you're thinking I'm crazy, that there's no way three is enough. When I first shared this methodology with Charlie, he said, "Michael, right now my team is quoting eight to ten prospects a day and not hitting goals. If I lower that to three, my team is going to maybe write a third of what they are now and they are already not hitting goals." On its face, that logic makes sense. But the big flaw in it is that it's predicated on the model of more. If your only approach to sales is More + More = More, then of course what Charlie said makes complete sense, and I'm the lunatic for proposing it.

But remember how I told you I was going to defy everything you had been taught about sales? The Model of More relies on numbers only. But the secret to sales success isn't about numbers. It's about people. It's about relationships. It's about solving problems. Let's actually break down and define what a quote/proposal looks like.

Real Conversations, Real Relationships

First you must actually *talk* to the prospect, not just email or text over some numbers. During this conversation, regardless of the industry you are in or whether it's over the phone, on a Zoom, or in-person, you must build rapport with the customer and get to know them. Then you must ask questions and have a discovery conversation with them. Then comes the proposal where you educate the customer and how your product/service solves their problem. Then lastly, you must ask for the sale. Yes, ask for payment information because you only help people if they actually buy from you. (I will break down this conversation in more detail later in the book.)

I went on to ask Charlie, "Out of the eight to ten quotes per person a day that your team is doing, how many of the prospects is your team actually having a conversation with and asking for the sale? How many prospects are they building a relationship with and discovering what kind of problems they have and why they are even shopping around for insurance?"

Charlie replied, "Zero." Just as I suspected.

I told Charlie, "Your team isn't quoting eight to ten people a day. They are quoting *zero* people a day."

Charlie's team was collecting information from a lead provider, using their quoting tools to put together a quote/proposal, emailing that over to the prospect, and *hoping* they were saving them money and the prospect would respond with a "Looks good, let's get it started." But the key word here is *hope*. Charlie's team wasn't actually employing any real sales skills or strategy. They weren't initiating any real business relationship. They were throwing some numbers at a wall *hoping* some stuck. This isn't an effective strategy. In fact, it's not a strategy at all. It's wishful thinking.

You see, Quote 3 puts an emphasis on what actually matters in sales, and that's having conversations, building relationships, solving problems, and asking for the sale.

Calls do not—let me repeat, *do not*—equate to sales. Conversations do!

Think about this for a moment. Let's say you're a financial planner and you had three appointments every day where you had real, in-depth conversations with prospects about their financial plan and their future. What would that do for your business and career? I can tell you what it would do—it would take off like a rocket!

If you are in life insurance sales and you sat down with three new prospects every day, discussed in detail what their current plan was for their family, and also discussed various unfortunate possibilities in life (such as sickness and unexpected deaths in the family and the impact that might have on family financial stability and security), what would that do for your business and career? I can tell you what it would do—you would be a Million Dollar Round Table (MDRT) agent making over seven figures a year!

Maybe you are in direct sales. What would it look like if you sat down with three people every day and asked sincerely what they wanted out of their life and how they planned on achieving their goals? And then if you explained how your product or service could help them do that? And then you taught your downline how to do the same thing? I will tell you what it would look like— you would be at the top of your company in less than a year!

I was recently talking to my speaking coach, Alex, and he was asking me what my new book was about. I said, "Before I answer your question, I have something on my mind: What would happen to your business if you spoke to three ideal customers a day and proposed your coaching services to them?" He responded with, "I wouldn't be able to handle the workload because I would have too many clients." I said, "That's exactly what my new book is about!" I then shared my Quote 3 methodology with him, and he loved it.

I can go on and on and on. It doesn't matter if you sell insurance, coaching services, cars, solar panels, or private jets, Quote 3 is the answer to solving your problem in sales. It makes you hyper-focused on what actually moves the needle, what moves your paycheck! It causes you to be super intentional with building relationships, discovering problems, and then solving those problems. With this approach, the only thing—and I mean the *only* thing—that matters daily is getting proposals out to three new prospects every single day. Think about how easy and simple that makes your life and sales career. You know every single day, you just come in and have meaningful conversations with three new prospects.

Most importantly, it forces you to slow down and have real conversations with people. You automatically become different from your competitors, and you automatically become customer-centric, which is exactly what you are supposed to do as a sales professional. Get to know your prospect, build commonalities with them, discover what struggles they are having and then educate them on how you can solve those problems with your product/ service. The best part is you only need to have three of these conversations a day to be wildly successful in your sales career.

When you begin doing this and implement not only this methodology but also the conversation I teach later, you will be closing one out of every three prospects you talk to. As you progress and become better at your craft and the conversation, you will be closing two out of every three prospects you talk to.

Right now I can see the doubt in your face. Charlie also gave me this same look and doubted me at first. He even told me, "Michael, this will never work. We won't be getting enough quotes out."

I replied, "I understand your skepticism, Charlie. I really do. But you are at a spot in your career where you are ready to give up and throw in the towel. What do you have to lose?"

Ninety days isn't going to ruin your career. We are talking about trying something new for ninety days. It's a tiny speck on the radar when looking at your thirty-plus year sales career. I am asking you to implement a strategy that has worked for over ten thousand sales professionals. The question is: If it has worked for ten thousand other sales professionals, why wouldn't it work for you?

Technology and the Future of Sales

It is my belief that we are at a pivotal point in sales and the future of sales. No matter what industry you are in, technology is going to have an impact on your industry and career. The good news with technology is that it is going to make your life easier as a sales professional. Prospecting will be easier. Servicing customers will be easier. It will be easier to utilize technology to enhance the overall customer experience!

However, when it comes to sales, technology also poses a threat. If a robot can do what you are doing, you will be replaced. Meaning that if you are planning on continuing to have transactional experiences with customers without building relationships and you refuse to have meaningful conversations, you will be replaced. Robots can crank out endless transactional quotes all day, every day—and they won't get tired, they won't get disillusioned, they won't get burnt out.

On the flipside, we are all becoming accustomed to more AI interactions in customer service. We all have to deal with robocalls and chatbots and AI customer service responding to our calls. There isn't a person on the planet at this point who hasn't said in exasperation and frustration, "I just want to talk to a real person!"

So transactional selling and buying using the *more* methodology may have worked in the past, but it will not work in the future. Your customers are wanting to have meaningful conversations. Your customers want to know they are taken care of. Your customers are wanting that go-to person who they trust and have a relationship with. For example, I just read a statistic from Charles Schwab that 83 percent of Generation Z want personalized advice from those individuals who they work with. This statistic is great news for you if you are willing to be the sales professional that I know you can be.

Quote 3 aligns perfectly with what customers want and expect out of you. Quote 3 makes the customer feel seen and heard. Quote 3 ensures that you build a relationship with the customer, discover their true needs and what they are looking for, and helps you propose your product or service in an educational and empowering way. Quote 3 replaces a transactional experience with a transformational experience allowing you to set yourself apart from the competition and position yourself as the go-to professional. Quote 3 not only sets you up for success, it also sets your customer up for success, while also making sure that you aren't replaced by technology in the future. You are in the people business; establish the human connection, make a difference, and get compensated handsomely for doing so. Not only will you get compensated, but you will also feel great about what you are doing for a living.

You should also know that your customer is willing to pay for the difference. According to *Forbes*, 86 percent of consumers say they are willing to pay more for a product or service if they find value in it. That's almost nine out of every ten consumers you talk to. You don't like being treated like a number and neither do your customers, and they are willing to pay for the difference for the value you provide them! But there's only value if you work with a model that allows you to have transformational interactions rather than transactional ones. The Quote 3 method is a proven approach that allows for just that.

When the Going Gets Tough, the Tough Stay Disciplined

Although Quote 3 is a straightforward method, that doesn't mean it's going to be easy to accomplish. You are going to have to prospect your ass off. There will be some days and weeks when you have to put in extra hours. There will be some days where you have no idea where the next conversation is going to come from, and you only have a few hours left in the day. You are going to get discouraged and want to quit. But that is part of sales and you signed up for it. You signed up for the most difficult, yet rewarding, career in the world. You get to help people, and you get the opportunity to make as much money as you want.

Quote 3 gives you a clearly defined target daily. You know exactly what you have to do to be successful to not only hit, but exceed your goals. But you still need to be fully committed and disciplined. This is why building your discipline starting with your morning routine is so important. You need to spend your days prospecting and filling your pipelines, getting appointments set. That means you need to avoid scrolling on social media for three to four hours daily like the average person does. You are going to have to be disciplined to not just sitting in front of your computer and checking your email every five minutes, looking like you are busy. You need to be disciplined to stick with activities that advance you further, that move the needle.

Here is the thing, you have total control of your future. You have total control of your career. You have total control of your life. You can continue to do what you are doing and getting the same results, or you can make the decision today to make a change and to actually start focusing on what is going to help you assist more customers so you can start making the money you want and living the life you want.

In case you need a bit more motivation, let me catch you up on where Charlie's at. He has now been utilizing the Quote 3 approach for the last two years. Not only did he implement this in his new business, but he also implemented it in his existing business. Over the last two years, his struggling new business went from almost shutting down to being a top 150 agency out of over twenty thousand insurance agents in the company he represents. His already existing business went from good to great! They are now a top fifty agency out of over twenty thousand in the company he works with.

He now has two thriving businesses and has increased his revenue by over $800,000 in the two years of adopting this methodology. Not only this, but prior to this approach, he had lost twenty-two employees over the previous three years between his two businesses. Since implementing Quote 3, his turnover decreased to only three people in the last two years.

You see, not only does your production and paychecks increase, Quote 3 provides clarity in how to win daily, which increases confidence and gives you and your team purpose. You actually feel *good* about what you do because you are having real conversations, solving real problems, and truly making a difference. This is what I call transformational selling instead of transactional selling!

The next thing we need to do is understand who your ideal customer is. (Yes, you control this too!)

CHAPTER
4

CREATING YOUR
IDEAL CUSTOMER

YOU WANT EVERYONE TO love what you sell. We all do. That's only natural. Being in sales we're helpers by nature. We are gratified to improve people's lives with what we can provide to them, but that doesn't mean we should try to sell to everyone all the time. Unfortunately, the Model of More has most sales people doing exactly this, which makes no sense.

Let's, for example, pretend you sell bread. Not only do you sell bread, but your bread is the best, specifically your banana nut bread. It's consistently voted #1 in every single competition you compete in. Everyone raves about your bread and how amazing it is. You approach my wife Courtney and start talking about your bread, how good it is, how it's consistently voted #1, and that she just has to have a piece. One major problem: Courtney can't have gluten. Courtney is *not* your ideal customer!

The point here is that because you were trying to enrich everyone's life with your bread—in this case my wife, Courtney— you ended up not only wasting Courtney's time, you wasted your time as well. Because as amazing as your bread is, Courtney is not going to be eating it. And that's just it—no matter how great your product or service is, it won't be for everyone. If you ignore this simple fact and try to indiscriminately sell to everyone, you're less efficient by design. You're dedicating time and resources to a segment of people who categorically will not want, need, or use your product. Knowing this and yet still trying to sell to them anyway is the definition of stupid. So why work stupid when we can work smart instead? Let's look at a few examples.

Let's say you sell private jet memberships with luxury flights, a full in-service menu, and comfortable seating options with flights that travel internationally out of all major airports. You have a great luxury product and service that a certain segment of the population will definitely find very attractive and very valuable. Your marketing strategy, however, targets everyone—meaning the person flying discount airlines, like Spirit, domestically and is looking for the cheapest flight from point A to point B is seeing your ads. This person is not your ideal customer, and never will be, but you're still churning through those marketing dollars putting your message out in front of them anyway.

Or maybe financial planning gets your juices flowing, which is why you got into the money game. You love to help people plan for retirement and invest their money. That's great. Your service is going to involve a weekly or monthly investment strategy to increase wealth and plan for future goals, like retirement. Your ideal customer, however, will not have the same or want the same strategy as someone who is focused on creating a budget to eliminate debt. If you are trying to sell your financial services for long-term financial planning and wealth generation to this person trying to pay off their credit card debt, you will be wasting your time and theirs. And there's always the unseen cost to wasting time: not only did you not close a new sale because you were pursuing a client who wasn't a good fit for your product or service, you were simultaneously missing out on an opportunity to be speaking with your ideal client who would very much want and benefit from your product or service.

It's not always so clear who your ideal customer is because obviously sometimes there's overlap in wants and needs. You may, for example, offer higher ticket offers for one-on-one in-person business coaching, but you consistently speak to prospects who are interested in working at their own pace in an on-demand virtual group setting that better aligns with their hectic schedules. It's not as if you would be completely off the mark here: the people you are speaking to do, in fact, want coaching services, but the method of delivery they seek is slightly different, which makes them not your ideal customer.

So the bottom line is that it doesn't matter if you sell insurance, business coaching, cars, or private jets, you must know exactly who your ideal customer is—but you need to put in the time to figure out who exactly they are. The biggest question with your ideal customer is, who do you want to serve and what problems do you want to help them solve?

To help you start thinking about your ideal customer, first I want you to think about everyone who is *not* your ideal customer. Who will *not* benefit from your product or service? Who *don't* you want to work with? Who do you not like working with or who is your product or service simply not a good fit for? Oftentimes this is easier than thinking about the perfect person.

For example, in my coaching and training business I have eliminated:

- Individuals who are near retirement and are no longer investing in their business or themselves.
- Individuals who aren't open to development and growth.
- Individuals who are happy with their income and complacent in their career.
- Individuals who view coaching and training as an expense instead of an investment.

Here are some examples of customer avatars I eliminated in the insurance business:

- Individuals who shopped insurance every six to twelve months.
- Individuals who only wanted the cheapest rate.
- Individuals who canceled insurance a month after getting it and only called to get their tags renewed.
- Individuals who only had one product to insure.
- Individuals with multiple claims or tickets on their record.

If you are a real estate agent, you might eliminate:

- Individuals with bad credit who can't get approved for a mortgage.
- Individuals who only believe in renting.
- Individuals who aren't employed.
- Individuals who are elderly and in a care facility.
- Individuals who have lived in the same house for over thirty years (they aren't moving anytime soon).

- Or maybe, depending on your space in the real estate market, you don't want to work with:
  o First-time homebuyers.
  o Anyone who can't purchase a $500,000+ home.
  o Homeowners at all (only investors).

If you are in car sales, maybe you could eliminate:

- Individuals with no income.
- Individuals with no credit.
- Individuals who live in the city and only walk or bike places.
- Individuals without a driver's license.
- Individuals who are elderly and no longer drive.
- Individuals that are tied to a brand that you don't offer. For example, you sell Fords and you come across a Jeep enthusiast. (That is basically like talking to a member of a cult; it's not going to happen, and they are definitely not your ideal customer.)

As you can see, figuring out who is *not* your ideal customer all depends on not only the field you're in, but also your personal specialty or expertise in the field, as well as the precise product or service you are selling. And it's important to think about this exercise as addition through subtraction. You're not eliminating prospects, you're instead gaining more time and resources to find and sell to the prospects who will actually want, need, and buy what you can provide them. Think about it this way: if you were a doctor who had really powerful medicine that could heal people who had a specific illness, you wouldn't want to waste your time and prolong the suffering of the people who are in need of your medicine by offering it to people who weren't sick and had no use for this amazing medicine. That would be ridiculous, almost criminal! Rather, you would do any and everything you could to find the people who needed your medicine the most, and part of that process would be identifying who wouldn't need it. It's the same thing here.

Once you eliminate who isn't your ideal customer, I want you to now get very specific on who *is* your ideal customer.

- How much money do they make?
- How old are they?
- Are they single or married?
- Do they rent or own their home?
- Do they have kids or not?
- What values do they have?
- Where do they live?
- What do they do for a career?
- What problems do they have?
- What pain do they face daily?

These are just a few that come to my mind. The more questions you can answer, the more specific you can get, the better. Your goal is to create the perfect customer avatar. Who is it specifically that you want to work with and *why* do you want to work with them? You need to think very deeply about this. Really spend some time being intentional about creating this person.

As a young sales professional selling insurance, I thought I could help everyone. *Everyone* needs insurance right? Wrong! I was writing a lot of business and helping everyone out who I came across and in contact with and then a few months later, people quit paying their bills, people were late on their bills, I was getting calls all the time about needing to suspend payments, and I was dealing with hundreds of small windshield and roadside service claims. Oh and I made a whopping $30 on average per customer I helped.

I was getting charged back money I had been paid because people weren't paying their bills. Now I was losing money. I was in my own personal hell and knew something had to change.

I did the exercise above that I am telling you to do. I created my ideal customer. My ideal customer:

- Was married.
- Was a homeowner.
- Made over $150,000 combined household income.
- Had kids.
- Owned two or more cars.
- Had a mortgage larger than $300,000 (this was in 2014).
- Liked extracurricular activities like traveling, working out, boating, or hunting.
- Was between twenty-five and forty-five years old.

I wanted to work with customers who I could help with financial planning, could use life insurance, had multiple items to insure, made enough money to pay the bills, and that I could work with for multiple years. I also wanted to work with people who I had things in common with. I also knew what problems these individuals had. They had assets that needed protecting; they needed their paychecks protected with disability and life insurance, so that in the event something happened they wouldn't lose everything that they had worked for; and they needed help with where to invest their money and creating a plan for retiring. In short, they needed an advisor who was looking out for their blind spots while they navigated life. I wanted to be that guy. I wanted to be *their* guy!

Once I created this ideal customer, everything changed. Let me be clear: this wasn't an overnight change or success. It took about ninety days of marketing and talking about the specific customers' problems before we started to see the work pay off. It was like magic though. We started helping out customers that fit this criteria. Not only did we help customers like this, we started attracting customers like this. Law of attraction was in full force. We would help one customer, and then they would refer us to a friend that was very similar to them. I went from being in my own personal hell to working with my dream clients! I was loving what I was doing, working with great people, and making a real difference in people's lives.

But that was only happening because I streamlined my energies to focus on the people I knew I could help the most. I didn't work more, I worked smarter. I dedicated my time, resources, and energies to finding prospects who would naturally benefit from what I had to offer. Once my prospects became stronger over time, my sales followed suit. One built upon the other in a perfect symbiotic relationship. Best of all, I was working *less* not more! But this all happened only because I knew who my ideal customer was.

Here's another example. Brandon is a friend and an insurance agency owner who I coach and work with. Much like my early years in insurance sales, Brandon was focused on writing anyone and everyone he could. He was frustrated. He was overwhelmed with the service and claims calls. He wasn't making the money he wanted to and was working much longer hours than he wanted just to keep his head above water every day. After having a conversation with Brandon, I told him things had to change and he had to get specific on who he wanted to work with and do business with. At first, he was skeptical, just like you might be. But he played along and did the exercise.

After we focused on the ideal customer avatar and created his ideal customer, it was time to turn on the marketing machine. (We'll discuss marketing in the next chapter.) Briefly though, this means it was time to speak to and attract his ideal customer so he could complete three conversations a day, every day, with his ideal customers.

Very similar to my results, it took about ninety days for Brandon to start seeing his work payoff. Just like me, those ideal customers started pouring in. He was helping more customers than ever, getting more referrals, and not having to work as much. His profitability increased year over year by 87 percent! Yes, 87 percent increase in pay. Not only has Brandon made more money, but he is in love with what he is doing again and looks forward to work.

So knowing your ideal customer is a critical component to being successful in sales. In a way, it's the catalyst for everything else because it helps you work smarter and more efficiently, which is what you need in order to create real relationships and have real conversations with prospects. The Quote 3 method is all about quality, not quantity. So you need to make sure that you are bringing in quality prospects day in and day out. That becomes a hell of a lot easier if you know what a quality customer is! Riches are in the niches, as they say, so the more specific you can be with your ideal customer and who you want to work with, the wealthier and happier you will be in your sales career.

CHAPTER
5

ATTRACTING YOUR IDEAL CUSTOMER

YOU HAVE YOUR IDEAL customer avatar created; now how the heck do you attract your ideal customer? That's what we're going to tackle in this chapter.

It was 2014 and, as you know, Courtney and I had just started our new business. The $5,000 we had saved wasn't going to go very far when it came to marketing and getting the word out that we were in business, so we had to think outside the box. Not only did we have our mouths to feed, we had already hired team members and told them we would provide them with leads to get started until they built a referral base.

I did what I did best—I hustled! I immediately signed up for the local Chamber of Commerce which over nine months led to a sum total of zero leads. I signed up for a direct mail campaign that would mail five thousand households in a ten-mile radius with information about our business. This led to another whopping total of zero leads. I instant messaged five hundred "friends" on Facebook, letting them know I had just opened up an insurance agency and would love to give them a free quote on their auto and home insurance which led to about twenty-five quotes. Then I called another lead company and struck a deal with them. The deal? They give me five thousand leads; I try them out; and if they were good leads and I had success, I would refer them to a minimum of twenty insurance agency owners, or else I would have to pay for the leads they gave me. I still am not sure to this day how I worked that deal, but they agreed to it. And after swinging and missing a number of times, we were finally in business!

We had five thousand names, addresses, emails, and phone numbers! Time to get to work. The team and I started pounding the phones, calling people who had no idea who we were. These were leads, but they were *extremely cold* leads. I had cold calling experience and was pretty good at it, but my new team had zero experience, and I knew there would be a learning curve. I took the challenge head on. I dialed my ass off from 8:30 a.m. until 8:30 p.m. I would get people interested and pass those on to the team. Then I'd hit the phones some more. That first month we wrote over 236 items and over $115,000 in premium. We crushed it!

My peers started to reach out and ask what I was doing because I was one of the top five agencies in the state of Missouri my first month in business. And just like that referrals were sent to the lead company, and they sent me fifty thousand more leads—for free! In our second month, we crushed it again. Month three, another repeat performance except by this time my team had figured out the cold calling game and were getting good at hitting their own quotas without me having to hand off leads. By this time, our social media presence, along with community presence with the events we were doing in the community finally started to pay off. Leads started to slowly but surely trickle in at a steady pace. We were off and running.

So how exactly did we convert extremely cold leads to winning business? How exactly did we generate steady six figure revenue from nothing in just a few months? In this chapter, I am going to cover strategies I have personally used that have worked for me and my sales teams many times. Everything from cold outreach to utilizing centers of influence to social media marketing to developing a hot leads list and more. I am going to supply you with multiple strategies and approaches. The entire purpose of this chapter is to teach you how to reach your ideal customer and keep your prospecting funnel open and running. I know I haven't said anything about referrals yet, but I dedicated the entire Chapter 7 to referrals.

You need to have multiple marketing strategies to ensure your prospecting funnels are full of ideal customers so that you are hitting your three quotes a day. This is what really matters when it comes down to it and what I want you to think about. What must you do to talk to three new prospects a day, every day? The first step is knowing who your ideal customer is. The next step is knowing how to reach them. This is where the marketing game comes in. You must have multiple strategies working for you to attract your ideal customer. Rather than spending entire days walking around a neighborhood, hoping someone's home, you can spend a couple of hours calling people and reach a ton more prospects, knowing all the while that they are "home," or they will be soon—because we live on our phones now!

Cold Outreach

Let's start by tackling cold outreach. When it comes to cold outreach, I am a huge fan of utilizing the phone. Yes, you can have automated email campaigns, which I would recommend as well. Sure, you could go door knocking, but how many doors can you actually knock on in a day? There are multiple strategies to cold outreach, but in my experience, nothing beats utilizing the phone by either calling or texting. People are on their phones for an average of two to three hours every day looking at social media, which means you already have a direct way to get their attention.

Cold calling campaigns can be very effective. What I recommend doing is working on a list of 250 to 500 names a month (or more if you can handle the workload yourself). On average, it takes eight calls per number to get someone on the phone, so I recommend twelve calls to each name before the end of the month. With 250 names times twelve calls, this equates to three thousand calls. When three thousand is divided by twenty working days, it equals 150 calls a day. Not only are you calling them twelve times, you are also emailing them and texting them (stay compliant within your state guidelines and rules). At a 10 percent conversation rate, which is what we typically experience, you are looking at twenty-five conversations. Out of twenty-five conversations, you are closing eight of them. Twenty-five conversations also gives you a little more than one quote/conversation a day when talking about twenty working days within a typical month. The better you get at your elevator pitch, the better your conversation ratio will be in turning contacts into quotes/conversations. (We'll cover the elevator pitch in the next chapter.)

In short, cold calling does work. The only people who say the phones are dead are those who either suck at calling or are trying to sell you on the newest and best marketing strategy that is sure to "make you rich and transform your business." Don't fall for it. Hitting the phones works now better than ever. Period.

That said, I don't want and wouldn't encourage cold calling to be your only strategy. It is just one strategy. I want you actively filling your pipeline and prospecting to ensure you get your three quotes in a day. This is a non-negotiable!

Part of your cold outreach should also include text messaging as I mentioned above. It's easier than ever to get in touch with prospects because their phone is always on them. Text messages average a 90 percent open rate within the first three minutes of texting someone! This is why when you are calling people you should also text them if they don't answer. You can also run text campaigns where you send out mass text messages to a large audience. Most Customer Relationship Management (CRM) systems and prospect management software systems have text capabilities.

The biggest tip I can give when sending a text message is to be short, sweet, and to the point, ensuring that your message will elicit a short answer that is easy for the prospect to give. For example, if you are trying to reach a prospect by the name of John, the first text I would recommend would be, "Hey, is this still John?" This will generate a quick yes or no. Either way, it will generate a response. If it's a yes, I recommend responding with, "I'm giving you a quick call," and as you press send, you call out! You know they have the phone in their hand and can talk; that is half the battle!

What not to do when it comes to text messaging is to send a mile-long text message about your product or service that you have to offer. That will generate absolutely no responses and they will report you as spam and block you immediately.

Another form of cold outreach is emailing cold prospects. These are prospects who have no idea who you are. Email outreach can be totally automated which is why I recommend it. Use technology to be more efficient and stay in front of prospects. Again most Customer Relationship Management systems have the ability to use automations and the capability to send mass emails to large audiences.

When it comes to email, conversion rates vary. I have found that emails have higher conversion rates in business-to-business (B2B) sales than it does in business-to-consumer (B2C) sales. For example, we average about a 13 to 15 percent response rate on emails to business professionals. When it comes to consumers, we average about a 5 to 7 percent response rate. Regardless if you are in B2B sales or B2C sales, I do believe that email marketing should be a part of your cold outreach plan, especially if you are calling or texting them. The more ways you have of reaching someone, the better.

Much like the text message, keep your email short, sweet, and to the point. Don't sound salesy and don't sound like you are from corporate America. One of my favorite emails is just putting in the subject line, "Did you get my voicemail?" or "Did you get my text message?" That's it, nothing in the body, and just pressing send. Or another one, "John, is this still your email?" Or if I am emailing a business owner after I have called their office, I will just send, "Did your team give you my message?" The entire point here is that you are looking to generate curiosity and a response.

Just like I said, don't make a text a mile long, don't make an email longer than two to three sentences at most. Again, you can also just use the subject line approach. Try multiple approaches and verbiage and see what gets the best response rate.

Centers of Influence

Now let's talk about centers of influence. These are people within your network who want to help you. They typically do business with you and have had success with your product or service and would be open to sharing their experience and recommend you to their network. These can also be friends who are in a business that you could create a referral relationship with. For example in the insurance space, I had real estate agents, mortgage brokers, and real estate investors who would send their customers and peers to me for business. These leads were typically *hot* leads that had high conversion rates (above 70 percent). This made total sense because someone they knew told them about me, how awesome my office was, and that they should be doing business with me. These, of course, are the types of leads you want, ones where you already are a recognized entity with the lead. You have instant credibility, so it's just a matter of showing how you can help them and closing the deal—high pay off in little time. Doesn't get any better than that.

For example, if you are a real estate agent, some centers of influence would be:

- Mortgage brokers
- Investors
- Insurance agents because they are always the first to know when someone is about to buy a house
- Financial planners because, much like insurance, they are going to work with clients to make sure they are prepared for home ownership
- Apartment complexes because when someone wants to go from renting to buying, you should be the first person on their mind to search for a home

So who could be a center of influence for you? Who has a giant network of individuals you can help? Who do you know who has influence within their space who you have helped with a product or service? Maybe you haven't helped someone of influence yet, so who could you help with your product or service who does have a large, extensive network?

Depending on the relationship you have with the different centers of influence, and if it's legal depending on the industry, they may want some kind of compensation, so just be prepared. If they do want compensation, remember that you are spending marketing dollars on extremely *warm*, if not *hot*, leads coming from a direct referral source! So in contrast to cold outreach, this is typically money well spent.

Social Media Marketing

Next let's talk about social media marketing. For many of you reading this, creating a brand on social media and being active is going to be an absolute must, a non-negotiable. This is the easiest way to get people to know who you are, what you do for a living, and—bonus—it is totally free! Use social media as a way to grow your network and educate your network on your product or service and what problems you solve. Knowing your ideal customer is key for social media because you need to know exactly who you are talking to and who you are attracting. A simple method to use is my 3x-3x-3x method:

- Grow your network by three new people every day
- Comment on three people's posts every day
- Make three posts a week

This is an easy way to grow and engage with your network and followers.

Pro tip: Don't just post content to post content. Make sure your content is relevant and is in line with your brand. Post content that is engaging and isn't solely focused on what you do for a living. Sure, you can and should have content around how you can help your audience and why people work with you, but you also need to post content that shows your audience who *you* are as a person. When you are in sales, you are in the people business. The more people can relate to you as a person (not just as a sales person), the better.

When it comes to social media, you can also actively prospect by sliding up in DMs. Although this strategy can be polarizing and many people may even try to shame you for it, I have no shame in my game. My goal is to help people, and the only way I am helping them is if they are working with me.

Don't get me wrong, I'm not advocating for any kind of shady, unethical behavior or business practices. I don't want you to DM someone and beat around the bush to just ambush them later. Be honest from the very start. Tell them what you do for a living and that you would love to help them out. For example, when I was in insurance and noticed a friend on social media was shopping for a new home, I would say something like:

> Hey (name), hope all is well. I noticed you are in the market for a new home, and I work at XYZ insurance company and specialize in working with homebuyers and would love to give you a free quote on some of the houses you are considering buying. When would be a good time to jump on a quick call and catch up?

You see, not sleazy at all. Direct and to the point. I personally received a lot of positive responses regardless of whether they wanted a quote or not.

Lastly, when talking about social media, paid ad campaigns can work really great in getting your information in front of your ideal customer and target audience. In my experience with paid ads, you will lose money until you figure out what ad hits and works. But once you figure it out, it can be a very lucrative approach. So for this strategy, it's especially important to know exactly who your ideal customer is so you can speak directly to them and the problem they have, which you can solve for them.

Money, Time, Skill

I have just covered some of my favorite marketing strategies that can lead to instant results and sales. There are, however, many more strategies—literally hundreds of different strategies you can use. Some are longer term strategies like billboards, snail mail, and ads on the tables of restaurants or shopping carts. These are all indirect marketing strategies that help create awareness of you and your product. The strategies I discussed in this chapter are more direct strategies that can and will equate to an immediate conversion and sale.

My personal favorite is cold calling. There is something about mastering your craft and learning human behavior and being able to convert *no's* into conversations. It's a challenge every single time and every single day. However, it can be extremely effective if you are willing to skill up, master your craft, and become a killer on the phone. I always said that if I learn to sell over the phone, I will never have to worry about money ever again in my life, and I still believe that today. The skills I have developed selling over the phone have not only carried me through rough patches, but have also contributed to building and growing multiple businesses.

In fact, cold calling has a special place in my heart because that is how we built our *first* business. Our back was against the wall, we only had $5,000 to our name, and we had to make things happen. We had bills to pay, we had a team to pay, our livelihood was on the line. Without the ability to develop a customer base through cold calling, we would have never made it. Which leads me to this, that all marketing strategies—regardless of what approach you're using—and how you acquire clients always comes down to three things: money, time, and skill.

You see, in the beginning of my career, we had very little money, so we could not spend a lot of money on other forms of marketing. We simply couldn't afford it. We did, however, have time and skill. I could work more hours, increase my skills, and master the art of selling on the phone. Through the years, not only did my skill continue to increase, my money increased, and that allowed me to use other forms of marketing to increase my reach, such as with paid ads and social media, which actually took very little time to do. This meant I could use money to buy back my time and increase the number of people who know who I am, which increased my lead generation and allowed me to stop making cold calls. With time, we also built a brand that generated enough referrals that I could completely stop all marketing spend, yet continue to have enough leads to meet and exceed our expectations every month.

The point here is, in the beginning of your career, you may have very little money, but you do have time and the ability to increase your skills. You need to utilize the variables you can control. You can compensate for a lack of money with time and the determination to hone your skills and develop your craft. You may have to do marketing strategies like cold calling, which may not be fun, but helps you get the job done. As time goes on, you increase your skills and start making more money. You can then use that money to market in different ways to buy back your time while increasing your sales volume at the same time. At the end of the day, we all start somewhere, typically at the bottom and to be able to get to where you are going, you have to put in your time, pay your dues, and grow yourself into the person it takes to make the money and have the life you want.

The benefit of the Quote 3 method and why it works so well is that it eliminates the lie of just do *more*. For example, when I started the insurance business, I would tell the team to just make *more* calls. "Focus on getting as many calls done a day," I would say. The problem, as I mentioned, is that's exactly what they did. They focused on calls instead of focusing on conversations, which is actually what matters. Quote 3 allows you to be hyper-focused on what actually matters in your marketing efforts and in sales. If you have three conversations a day, where you are building a relationship, discovering problems, proposing your product, and asking for the sale, you are going to be wildly successful in your sales career.

To conclude this chapter, please remember that marketing is a must. You always have to be growing your network and creating awareness around what you do for a living and how you can help your ideal customer. You must do whatever it takes to consistently fill your prospecting pipeline so that you can talk to three new people every single day about your product or service and how you can help them. Quote 3 only works if you work. Prospecting and marketing is how you get the leads and people to talk to.

6

THE QUOTE 3 CONVERSATION

OKAY, WE'VE DISCUSSED THE importance of discipline and having a personal routine and how that is a competitive advantage. I walked you through the Quote 3 method and the importance of accomplishing three quotes/proposals a day. We have covered who your ideal customer is and strategies to get them into your prospecting funnel. But what do you do then? It's one thing to have a solid lead; it's another thing entirely to close that lead. So the conversation with the prospect is where it's at. This is where the magic happens. The conversation is what turns prospects into paying customers.

This is exactly what I am going to cover in this chapter. This conversation has been taught to and adopted by over ten thousand sales professionals across the country, ranging from insurance sales to coaching services and from financial advisors to those in direct sales with multi-level marketing companies.

But before we get into the framework of the conversation, I want to introduce you to Kat. Kat worked with an insurance agency owner who had hired me to help their team. Kat was a sales producer who had been working in the agency for a couple of years prior to us working together. At that point, she was an average producer. However, she was young, ambitious, and hungry! She not only wanted to do better, she knew she was capable of doing better.

In talking with Kat, she wasn't satisfied with her current production at all. Sound familiar, my fellow high achievers? Sure, she was the top producer in her agency, but as I have already stated, she was ambitious and ready to take things to the next level. As I was talking to Kat about her goals—key performance indicators, time management, and others—I just happened to ask her how she was feeling about what she did for a living as an insurance professional. At first, I received the typical high-level response of, "It's great!" She sounded like me when I was younger and just getting into my career, "It's great, everything is great, nothing but good stuff going on over here."

I decided to dig in. "Tell me what 'great' feels like," I said. Just like that, Kat got a little uncomfortable, and I could tell on the virtual call the question caused her to squirm a bit.

Kat responded, "How it feels?"

"Yes," I replied. "I want to know how what you do every day makes you feel great."

Kat paused and then said, "I love working here and with my agent and teammates. I have learned so much and feel like I am just getting started and have so much more to learn. *But* I'm not as energized and fired up as I used to be about what I'm doing. Sure,

I hit the goals every month and usually exceed the goals, but I got into this business to change lives and help people, and I feel like I am just going through the motions and some days feel like I'm just a product pusher."

Wow! I thought to myself. *This girl is a potential rockstar, and she is unfulfilled and on the verge of burnout.*

Can you relate to Kat at all? I know throughout my sales career, I had these same feelings creep up multiple times, and I could feel deeply for Kat and understand exactly what she was going through and how she was feeling. I remember being new to sales, just trying to hit goals so my paycheck would be big enough to pay the bills. I was focused on whatever I could do to be at the top of the chart every month, just concentrating on getting the sale and moving on to the next customer.

Here is what I realized: if you are just focused on the next sale, focused on the next call, focused on the next activity, there is absolutely nothing fulfilling about the job. So when I was talking to Kat and heard the words coming out of her mouth, I knew the Quote 3 method was going to not only be a perfect fit for her, but also a must for her to sustain her career as a sales professional.

I decided to dig in a little more and ask her what a typical quote/proposal meant to her.

She responded with, "I typically put a quote together based on the information provided, email and text the quote over to the prospect, and then give them a call to see what they think."

"So you're hoping you save them money and they say yes?" I replied.

She responded with a simple, "Yes."

"What happens if you don't save them money?" I asked.

"Well, then they typically respond with a *no* or *no thank you*," she said.

"All right, last question, Kat. If you're wanting to change people's lives, why are you emailing them quotes and hoping you save them money instead of having conversation with them about their problems, why they are shopping for insurance in the first place, and what they are looking for out of an insurance agent they do business with? What is important to them? What problems do they have that you can solve?"

"I don't know how to have a conversation like that."

And there it was, just like that, we discovered the underlying problem. Kat wasn't confident in what a sales conversation should sound like. Her entire method up until this point was hoping and praying she saved a prospect money on their insurance. This method is part of the problem with the lie you have been sold with the Model of More approach, which says, "If you talk to enough people, eventually you'll get a yes." Awful. This is awful advice.

As problem solvers, we need to be connecting with people, relating to people, and understanding who they are and what they need to make their lives better. This requires a conversation. A real conversation. And that's what I'm about to share with you. The framework for how a real conversation should look and feel. Something that, of course, has some parameters and guidelines, but is still real and authentic.

The Quote 3 conversation will help you achieve above a 30 percent closing ratio on cold business and above a 60 percent closing ratio on referral business. That's right, you are about to start closing one deal a day, every single day when you start implementing the Quote 3 conversation into your business practice.

Let's get into it. The conversation is comprised of five parts:

- Conversation Starter
- Rapport Building
- Discovery Conversation

- Proposal
- The Close

We will look closely at each component of the Quote 3 conversation, so we can see what's entailed in each specific part and also see how each part builds and works off the part that precedes it. As you become familiar and comfortable with each component of the conversation, the parts will all begin to blend seamlessly into one—and your sales will start skyrocketing.

The Conversation Starter

The conversation starter is where it all begins, hence the name. It's your elevator pitch. Now depending on if you are in B2B (business-to-business) sales or B2C (business-to-consumer) sales, and depending on if you're selling a service or a product, your conversation starter is going to vary somewhat. But this framework will help you create an elevator pitch that will be very effective in helping you turn more contacts into customers regardless of the type of sales you do or what it is you're selling.

The Who

The first part of the conversation starter is *who*. Who are you? What is your name and what company do you represent? An example of this would be as follows:

> "Hey John, Michael Weaver here with XYZ insurance company."

> Or maybe you sell cars, "Hey John, Michael Weaver here with XYZ auto dealer in town."

This is a very simple step, and although simple, it is critical in the conversation. Within the first three to five seconds of the conversation, you have clearly stated your name and company.

Pro tip 1: Always call the prospect by their first name. No last name and no Mr. or Mrs. Using a person's first name automatically personalizes the connection to some degree. Addressing them by their first name signals that you see them and you recognize them as a person, as would a person they already know and are familiar with. So, in effect, it breaks through that initial "stranger/ unknown" wall. Using surnames is stiffer and more formal, so it keeps you squarely in the "sales person" realm to them, and the call remains colder and more distant as a result. People are more apt to go along with people they know and trust, and addressing people by their first name puts you in that zone within the first few seconds of the call.

Pro tip 2: Tonality matters. You have less than fifteen seconds before someone decides whether they like you and are going to have a conversation with you. You want to sound relatable, not salesy. Quit trying to sound a "certain way" and be yourself. Think of a prospect as the same as talking to a friend, an old co-worker, a family member, or an old classmate who you haven't talked to in a few years. The less salesy you sound and more genuine and authentic you are, the more success you are going to have.

The What

Now after the Who, we have the What. *What* do you do or offer? This is your product or service you provide. Example:

> "Hey John, Michael Weaver here with XYZ insurance company calling about your auto and home insurance."

As a consumer, John now knows your name, company, and what you are calling about. This has all happened within the first six to eight seconds. Clear and concise.

The Why

Next is the most important part, the Why. *Why* should they give you the time of day in the first place? This is your big, BOLD statement. Here is the thing, you have less than fifteen seconds to get it out, so it must be to the point. This is your attention grabber. Here's an example that builds from the earlier ones:

> "Hey John, Michael Weaver here with XYZ insurance company calling about your auto and home insurance. Your rates just increased, and I have been able to help the last nine out of ten people I have talked to."

I want you to read that starter out loud. Twelve seconds, twelve! That's it. That's all it took to fully articulate my BOLD statement. And this is just one example of a bold statement. You may "save customers $X amount on average" or be "voted #1 in customer satisfaction" or "increase revenue by X in X days."

Depending on your service/product, your bold statement will be different and unique to you and unique to your prospect and how you can help them. Your BOLD statement needs to be bold, but also true. Don't make false statements just to grab someone's attention. If you are willing to lie then, you are willing to lie at all times, and you will eventually get caught!

Assume the Conversation

The last part of the conversation starter is the assumption of the conversation. This is your bridge to engaging the prospect. After you clearly state your BOLD statement, you go straight into the conversation:

> "Hey John, Michael Weaver here with XYZ insurance company calling about your auto and home insurance. Your rates just increased, and I have been able to help the last nine out of ten people I have talked to. Tell me, is your address still 123 Main Street?"

See how I just assumed the conversation by asking the address? Asking a question—and especially a question that is easy for the person to answer—necessarily gets them into a conversation with me. Once you cross that bridge, it's much easier to keep going.

Other examples of good easy questions to bring people into a conversation might be "So, how long have you owned the business?" or "How many people do you have on your sales team?"

Again, these are simple questions to ask and answer. Address, years in business, number of sales team members—all would be easy recall questions for someone. It gets them talking and gets you into a conversation.

Assumption is critical here. Your job as the sales professional is to make it easy on your prospect, so simplicity is the key. The simpler the better. And the better you get at assuming the conversation, the more success you will have as a sales professional.

Pro tip: Be enthusiastic! The more enthusiastic you are, the more excited the prospect will be, hence the old saying, "Smile through the phone."

Overcoming Objections

I've just covered how to create your conversation starter, but I wouldn't be doing you justice if I didn't talk about being ready to overcome objections. You are going to receive objections. That's just part of the business. And they will come in many forms, so you need to be familiar with them. Here are just a few examples:

- "I don't have time."
- "I went with someone else."
- "I'm good where I'm at."
- "How did you get my information?"
- "What's the price?"

I could go on for days with different objections you could potentially receive. When thinking about objections, the first thing I would tell you to do is track the objections you are hearing. Meaning for a two-to-three-week timeframe, write down every objection you hear in your conversation starter. This is going to provide you with some much-needed data. After you compile your data, you are going to realize you are hearing the same four to five objections most often. These are the objections you are going to need to prepare most for and become great at overcoming.

A simple framework for overcoming initial objections is using the AAA method. AAA stands for Agree, Address, and Assume.

Let's start with the first A: Agree. While you may not agree completely, you never want to come across as combative or argumentative in the sales conversation. So instead you say something that suggests empathy and understanding, something like "I'm with you" or "I understand" or "I get it." This helps the prospect on the other end of the phone or across the table feel seen and heard. That is step one! Always agree!

The next A is Address. You want to address the objection. For example, let's say that a prospect answers the phone, you go through your elevator pitch, and they say, "I'm busy." You would then respond with:

> "I'm with you, John, I know that you are busy."
> (We aren't done yet, though!)

You see what we did there? We agreed with the prospect and then addressed his objection.

Now it's time for the last A; it's time to Assume! Assuming is a big part of getting the initial conversation started and just as important in overcoming objections. After you agree with the customer, address the objection, you are then going to assume the conversation and get right back to the sales process. For example, to complete what we started above, you might say something like the following:

> "I'm with you, John, I know that you are busy.
> The best part is, I just need a few minutes of your
> time today. So tell me..."

You see how that worked? I agreed with the customer, addressed the objection, and then assumed they wanted to continue the conversation with me. The trick here is to, again, go for an easy *yes*. Make it easy on the prospect—especially now that you know they are resistant or hesitant after putting up an objection. Ask them something that requires an easy answer and will end with yes. Here are some different easy questions based on various sales fields:

- If you are in insurance, you could say:

"So tell me, is your address still 123 Main Street?" or "So tell me, do you still drive the 2021 Chevy?" (This is information you would have in front of you).

- If you are a real estate agent, you could say:
  "So tell me, it looks like your address is 123 Main Street. Is that right?" or "So tell me, it looks like you have lived at this property for about five years. Is that correct?

- If you are in car sales, you could say:
  "So tell me, it looks like you bought the Chevy from us three years ago. Does that sound right?" or "So tell me, it looks like your address we have on file is 123 Main Street, is that still correct?"

Pro tip 1: The better you get at assuming the conversation, the more objections you will overcome and the more conversations you will have—meaning the faster you will accomplish your three quotes for the day!

Pro tip 2: After going for the immediate yes, then start to build rapport and ask an open-ended question. (We'll cover rapport later in this chapter.)

Another form of the AAA method is a technique called the "Feel, Felt, Found" method. This technique has been around since the beginning of time, I think. I first learned this technique when I was twenty-two years old, and I was listening to Brian Tracy. Why is this a big deal? Because Brian Tracy is the OG of sales training! The "Feel, Felt, Found" method goes as follows:

"I understand how you *feel*. Many of our current clients *felt* the same way and told me the same thing; however, what they *found* was that by giving me just a few minutes of their time, I was able to help them out, and now they are happy customers of mine. So tell me…"

It's easy to notice the similarities with AAA, but with this variation, we more explicitly tell the prospect that we relate to their feeling, and through relating to them, we can also reassure them that they won't feel this way for long—because what we have to offer will change everything. We are then back to assuming the conversation once more.

Pro tip: Always start the conversation with the end in mind. The end is, they are a paying customer. For them to become a paying customer, they have to have a conversation with you. You are never going to ask if they want to have a conversation with you. You assume they want to be part of that conversation. Always assume!

Don't let objections scare you or worry you. Track your data, create the framework for overcoming the objections you hear most often, practice with your teammates, and then implement and use on prospects.

Rapport Building

Now, let's get on to the second stage of the conversation. This step is called the Rapport Building phase!

This stage of the conversation is oftentimes overlooked and skipped in the sales process. So many times sales producers want to get straight to the product/service they are offering. The problem here is that people buy and do business with those who they know, like, and trust. Although real trust takes time, there is going to have to be a base level of trust to give you payment information. By building rapport with a customer, you are going to discover commonalities with them and things you have in common.

First, if you don't know what rapport is, rapport is defined as, "a close and harmonious relationship in which the people or groups concerned understand each other's feelings or ideas, and communicate well," according to the American Society of Administrative Professionals.

In simple terms, rapport is asking questions and getting to know the individual you are talking to on more of a personal level. A simple framework for building rapport that you can use is FOR:

F – Family
O – Occupation
R – Recreation

What does this mean exactly? These are the three domains you can use to converse with your prospects to build rapport. Notice that each of these are safe categories, ones that your prospect typically has love for and intimate connections to and that should also be non-controversial. There's a reason the acronym isn't PRT—Politics, Religion, and Taxes.

You can target the FOR domains to enter into a more informal, personalized exchange with your prospect that will start to create commonalities, which in turn will build more trust. You can also tailor what domain you choose based on who your client is. If you get the sense your prospect is more family-oriented, you can dip into the family domain. If the prospect is giving off a passionate vibe about their business or career, you can venture into the occupation category. Or if they happen to mention something that they do on the side—skiing, working out, avid reader, or other activities—you can try to make a connection on the recreation front. Below are some quick and simple examples of questions you can ask:

When asking about family:

- Are you married?
- Do you have children?
- Do you have relatives in the area?

When talking about their occupation:

- What do you do for a living? Where do you work?
- How long have you worked there?
- Do you work remotely or in the office?
- What do you enjoy about what you do?

When discussing recreation:

- What do you do when you aren't working?
- Do you have any travel plans in the near future?
- Do your kids play sports?
- Do you have any hobbies?

These are just a few examples of questions to ask and topics to discuss. Ask them questions, get to know them, get them talking, and find out things that you have in common with them. This will make you relatable which will help establish the like, know, and trust factor.

Pro tip 1: The more they talk, the more they like you. Everyone likes to talk about themselves, and people are flattered (even if they're not consciously aware of it) when people show interest in things they say. So ask questions, and let them talk away!

Pro tip 2: Be engaged and curious. When they answer a question dig into the answer by using a simple phrase like, "Tell me more about that" or "That's so interesting. How does that work?" People like to feel seen and heard. Asking additional questions accomplishes this goal. But it's important to do so genuinely. Be authentic in your engagement. Be real in your curiosity.

Pro tip 2: When asking a question and someone responds with an answer, wait two to three seconds to respond. This will give them plenty of time to make sure they have got their complete thought out and give you time to process and respond.

You may at this point be saying to yourself, "Michael, this is *a lot*. I don't have the time for this." The best part about building rapport and finding commonalities that makes you more relatable is that it happens much quicker than you think. In most conversations, the rapport phase will only last five to ten minutes. That's it! The five to ten minutes of rapport building time is critical to your success and an absolute must.

The more you have in common, the more relatable you are, the more they like you, the higher your chances are of turning them into a paying customer. Since 96 percent of people buy on emotion, a big part of that emotion is going to be how they feel about you.

Discovery Conversation

Next, we have the discovery phase of the conversation. The discovery phase of the conversation is where you discover the prospect's hot button/pain point. This is where you *discover* the problems they are having and what they are currently struggling with. Why are they shopping? Why are they talking to you today? This portion of the conversation is where they, as well as you, discover how your product/service is going to help them.

Every stage of the conversation is important, but this one stands out to me because this is where you as the sales professional have to get really good at asking questions and then also *listening* to the prospects answer, which you then use to ask more questions to probe even deeper into their pain points in order to determine what they really need and how you can solve their problems. Remember, 96 percent of buyers buy on emotion, and the discovery phase of the conversation is what triggers that initial emotion. That is, it's the pain they are feeling and how their struggles are affecting them, emotionally, physically, and financially.

This portion of the conversation should last ten to fifteen minutes for most sales professionals in most industries. Now I want to dive into this a little because every industry is a little different. The more expensive your product or service is, generally the longer the discovery conversation is—not in all cases but most, in my experience.

For example, if you are in insurance and having a conversation with a prospect about their auto and home insurance, you can find out in about five to ten minutes what's important to them, what their problems are that they want solved, and what they are going to expect out of you as their insurance agent.

If you are in the coaching industry and your one-on-one coaching product costs $120,000 a year, a discovery conversation is going to be much longer than five to ten minutes. That discovery conversation is going to be deeper and would last about thirty to forty-five minutes. The point is that the discovery conversation will vary to some degree but is absolutely vital to sales success, so gauge how long it should be based on your industry and the type of product or service you are selling.

The better you get at the discovery conversation and figuring out the customer's pain, the higher your closing ratio will be. This is the phase where you determine how you are going to craft your proposal based on the customer's problems and needs.

There are three questions that need to be answered during the discovery conversation:

- Are they your ideal customer?
- Do you align with them?
- Can you fix their problem?

The answer needs to be *yes* to all three to be able to proceed with the conversation and before you move into the product/service proposal.

You may be saying to yourself, "This is great and all, but how do I even start this conversation?"

This is a valid question. One of my favorite ways to open this conversation is by simply saying, "Now I'm going to ask you a few questions to get to know your situation a little more and what's important to you. Just as importantly, I want to make sure that my product/service is a good fit for you and can solve your problem. So tell me...."

Using this framework is a great way to start the conversation. Then when they begin talking, use those two ears you were born with and listen. *Really* listen, not only to what they are saying but perhaps also to what they are not saying, what they are not telling you. The prospect will try to keep the conversation high level and give you short answers—one- and two-word answers if possible. It is your job to dig in and get them talking. Remember the phrase I shared with you just a little earlier, "Tell me more about that"— this is a critical phrase during this part.

Once you uncover one problem, dig in for another! Try to find a minimum of two to three pain points and struggles. The more problems your prospect has, the more pain they have, and the higher the buying momentum is. Without discovering the prospects problem, you don't know what's important to them or how you can help them.

How can you propose your product/service without first having this conversation? Simple: you can't!

If you are like many sales professionals I have worked with, if you aren't having this conversation, you are struggling hitting goals consistently. You're living paycheck to paycheck, and you're unfulfilled in what you are doing.

I know what I am asking you to do may sound scary. I know it's going to challenge you and your beliefs. I know it's easier to assume your prospect's problems. I know it's easier to tell them about your products and *hope* you save them money.

But the discovery conversation takes you from being an amateur to a professional. It takes you from being a transactional salesperson to being a transformational sales professional where you actually feel good about what you're doing. You feel fulfilled because you are having a meaningful conversation with people daily, solving problems. This simple but vital step will help you increase your closing ratio, so you help more people and make more money.

Pro tip: Be an active listener. I want to dive into this for just a moment because I believe this is a skill that gets overlooked in most sales industries. What does being an active listener mean? Well, being an active listener is part of being engaged and curious—that is, you are asking questions to learn about the prospect, their situation, and what they are telling you, as we discussed in the Rapport Building section of the conversation. When you receive an answer, you ask another question about what they just told you. You dig into their answers and have them explain in more detail what they mean. Why I want to address this here is because so many times when we as salespeople ask prospects questions, we tend to ask the question not to listen but to then respond with what else we need to say or just move on to the next question in the conversation. I was absolutely guilty of this very early on in my sales career. Actually, not only my sales career, but even when talking to family or friends. I would ask a question, they would respond, and then I would just start talking again or ask another question about something that had nothing to do with what they just told me. But building trust and truly getting to know the pain points of your prospect is critical during the discovery phase of the conversation. So your ability to actively listen and engage your prospect is vital. The best sales professionals in the world ask great questions, listen, and then ask more great questions. The less you talk as the sales professional, the more successful you are going to be in your sales career.

Sometimes it's hard to break old habits, though, especially in the moment. So a strategy for active listening is, yes, to ask great questions, but another aspect of active listening is to *reflect* back to the person what they just told you. This is a simple technique that shows (a) you actually listened to and heard what the person said, and (b) you are actually taking the time to confirm with them that you heard them correctly. Both are crucial to establishing a clear line of communication and trust during the discovery conversation. The technique of "reflecting" is essentially repeating back or paraphrasing what someone says. So after you ask a question and listen to a prospect's answer, you would reply with something like "So what I hear you saying is..." or "Correct me if I'm wrong, but it sounds like you are saying..." Implementing active listening techniques such as this also has the added benefit of helping you slow yourself down. So if you're prone to just moving on to the next item in your agenda, taking time to actively reflect back the thoughts and replies of your prospect necessarily helps you avoid rushing through the conversation, which is the last thing you want to do during the discovery conversation. What comes of all this is an experience that is more rewarding for both you and the prospect.

The Proposal

Now it's time for the next step of the conversation, the proposal!

The proposal is your time to shine! This is what all of your hard work has led to. You have taken the time to get to know your prospect. You have built rapport and established commonalities with them. You have discovered their problems and struggles. You now understand *why* they are shopping and *what* they are looking for. It's now time to do what you do best. It's time for you to educate your prospect on how your product/service solves their problem.

Your proposal needs to be well thought out and specifically address the prospect's pain point. It needs to be educational, informative, and include stories that they can *see* and relate to. It needs to empower the prospect. Your proposal should clearly paint a picture for the prospect of what your product does for them, why it's a great fit for them, and how you have helped customers just like them.

Remember to Keep Asking Questions!

Depending on your product or service, your proposal could be ten minutes long or it could be thirty minutes long. It will vary. Most importantly, it needs to speak specifically to the prospect's issues and keep your prospect engaged and involved in the conversation, so they aren't just sitting there listening to you. This is to say, it can't just be a lecture.

Think back to when you were in school or college. After a few minutes of your instructor talking, how often did you sit there in rapt attention, hanging on their every word? Or after a minute or two, were you more likely to zone out, check the clock, your phone, what was going on outside the window—doing anything but listening to the person droning on and on with no regard for you and no idea how boring they were? My guess—and the experience of 95 percent of students of *everywhere*—is the latter. No one wants to be lectured, so don't do it to your prospects or customers!

Be informative but concise. Make sure you are continually engaging them. One easy way to do this is by asking confirmation questions like:

- "Does that make sense?"
- "How do you feel about that?"
- "Would you agree this is a good fit for you?"

To be clear, this is a good start, but that's not enough by itself. These questions can lead to one word, polite, almost robotic answers—"Yes," "Good," "Sure." That's not enough. So these are good lead questions, primer questions, but you need to follow up to really keep them involved and actively engaged in a dialogue with you. If you ask a question that goes for a "Yes," such as, "Does that make sense?" I want you to follow the *yes* up with a "Tell me more about that and how it makes sense for your situation."

Make them tell you what *is* making sense *or* why they agree that your product/service is a great fit, *or* why it is not if they say no. By doing this, you are having the prospect verbally process and tell you how your product/service not only fixes their problems, but also why it's a better fit for them. Or you're having them verbally process and present to you why it's not, which allows you time and the opportunity to ask more questions to discover what they are looking for based on what they say. Either way, engagement such as this during the proposal phase keeps the needle pushing forward because the longer you are conversing, the longer they are engaged, the higher your probability is of getting to close.

Pro tip: Using confirmation questions throughout the conversation is a form of closing technique called the ascending close. I also refer to this as the bobblehead close. By asking confirmation questions, you are getting the prospect to agree with you that this product is a great fit for them and solves their problem. They just keep saying *yes*. Imagine driving down the road with a bobblehead, and its head just nods up and down—that's exactly what you want your prospect doing so that when you get to the close, they are used to saying *yes*!

Obviously during the proposal, you do typically talk more than the prospect. But you need to always remember this core sales maxim: telling is not selling. Asking questions is a must during this process.

So with that all said, I want to help you with structuring and organizing your proposal.

First, let's determine what problems you solve. What three to five specific problems does your product/service solve for most customers? Maybe you save them time, make them more money, help them with accountability, or provide financial security. Whatever it is, you need to be crystal clear as to *how* and *why* you can solve your prospect's problem.

An easy example to share is how we help insurance producers. One product saves insurance agency owners time and training resources by teaching their new insurance sales producers how to begin closing deals within ten days of starting their career. Then we teach them how to make six figures as an insurance sales producer over the following eight weeks. In short, their problem? Training new hires to generate clients and revenue for the firm. Our solution? We do the onboarding and sales training for them! Not only does this save them time, it ultimately saves them money by shortening the training overhead and giving them a consistent process for their business that begins to generate real revenue sooner than later.

Another product we offer makes insurance producers instant money by teaching them how to write thirty or more life insurance policies in just five days. It teaches them how to start the conversation, how to have a life insurance conversation, and then how to ask for the sale. This increases their confidence and teaches them the proven strategies and processes it takes to be a high performer and sales producer. Plus, they get instant wins and make money quickly! This is a spectacular return on their investment (ROI).

These are just two examples of how we specifically address our customers' most common problems and struggles. So let's go back to what your product/service solves for your customers. Remember to speak directly to how you solve your prospects' problems.

Stories Sell!

Next, I want you to think about your current customers and how you have helped them. What successes have they had by using your product service? What am I getting at? Stories!

Stories are powerful. We live, breathe, and relate to stories. What do you do on your downtime? You read a book. You watch a movie. You stream a show. About what? People's lives. Doesn't matter if they're real or fake. We gravitate to and are affected by stories. And the stories we gravitate to the most are about characters we relate to the most and stories that we find the most inspiring.

Sometimes it's easier to make this point clearer by looking at the opposite. Think of movies you watch over and over again. What are the common themes? The two lovers get together in the end. The underdog triumphs over all odds. The good guys win over the bad guys.

Now think about movies that you actually might have liked but you never watched again—and never want to. My bet is that the lovers did *not* get together in the end, or the underdog came close but actually didn't win (think *Rocky* vs. *Rocky II*), or the character or characters you loved died right before the credits rolled. You can appreciate those movies, those stories, but you don't *love* them. You don't want to revisit them over and over again. Why? They're not inspiring. They're slightly depressing. They're slightly de-motivating.

The point is, stories are crucial because they sway people's emotions, which is exactly why it's so important that you not only tell stories but that you choose the *right* stories to tell. The stories you choose have to be genuine, authentic, and moving in some way. Ideally, the stories would have some personal meaning or significance to you. These are the types of stories that move people to act. The things that move us in our lives are not statistics, numbers, or theories. We are moved and touched by the stories and lives of other people.

So, for example, incorporating client *success* stories into your proposal is a must. The stories don't have to be long; thirty to forty-five seconds is great. You also don't need a thousand stories to share. Just one or two stories of customers you currently work with and have helped that were similar to your prospect and faced similar problems is plenty. Incorporating client success stories into your proposal will allow the prospect to better understand how your product or service is going to solve their problem and give them confidence that your product or service is going to work in the same way because you have helped someone just like them in a similar situation. Here's an example of a personal story I have.

I woke up to a text that read, "Mike, Drew died last night on his way home from work, and I was reaching out to see if you knew if he had any life insurance with you." Drew was a buddy of mine from high school that was also a client I worked with in insurance. I instantly walked to the shower, turned it on, stepped inside, and just stood there thinking, *Fuck, fuck, fuck, fuck.* Tears started to roll down my face. I knew he didn't have any life insurance.

Early in my career, I had a conversation about life insurance with Drew after he had his first kid, and he said, "Nah, Mike, I got something through work. Plus, nothing's going to happen to me!" I knew what his work policy was like—and it wasn't good at all. With Drew being a friend, though, I didn't press it. We cracked a couple more jokes and went on our separate ways.

A couple of years later, he had another kid, and I didn't bring it up because he had already told me no, and I didn't want to be "that guy" that bothered my friends about life insurance. But that morning in the shower, all I could think about was how I didn't ask Drew about life insurance ever again, and now he has a wife, a three-year-old, and six-month-old who will only receive $50,000 in life insurance and most of that will go to burial costs and medical bills. I was absolutely devastated. It shook me to my core. I let Drew down, I let his family down, and now they were going to have to suffer financially. Because I didn't do my job, Drew's wife had to sell their home, move in with her parents, and struggled financially for multiple years after Drew's death.

It was on that day that I made an agreement with myself to ask every single prospect and client I talk to about their insurance plan, and I always shared Drew's story. To this day and even as I type this, I get emotional thinking about this situation with Drew and his family. This is a story I share when I coach and train life insurance professionals, and every single time I get choked up. I share it to remind them how important of a career they have, the difference they can make, and the importance of asking every customer every time about life insurance because I never want them to be in the situation I was in, standing in the shower, knowing I didn't do my job, and now a family had to suffer financially because of it.

This may not be a client success story, but it is a personal story and a powerful story that I hope shows you how important stories are in a sales conversation. This is why you get into sales in the first place: to change people's lives.

The Perfect Fit: Value Statements

We have now discussed the importance of educating your prospect on your product or service and how it fixes their problem. We have also discussed the importance of incorporating stories into the conversation. The final piece of the proposal is about you and your company and how you are a great fit for them and how you are different than your competitors. This is what I call the value statements portion of the proposal.

- How are you going to serve the customers with on-going customer service?
- What can they expect from you or your team when they call in the future?
- What do you do that aligns with what they are looking for, not only now but in the future?
- Why you? Why your company? Why your product/service?

I want you to come up with three to five value statements that align with the most common customer you work with. Not only should you come up with these statements, but you should also ask yourself, how can you incorporate these into the stories that you share?

Now that you have all the steps to the proposal, we are on to the final step and stage of the conversation, the close!

The Close

The Close is where it is time to ask for money. The close is where you actually help your prospect. This is where you convert the prospect you might be able to help to a customer that you definitely will help.

Most importantly, the close is where you make money!

Assume the Sale

Just like the line made famous from the movie *Jerry Maguire*, it's time to "Show me the money!" It's officially time to ask for payment details. How do you do that? Well, you have to be a bit more blunt in this phase. You basically have to come out and just say:

- "Are you putting this on your Visa or AMEX?"
- "What payment plan works best for you?"
- "To get this started, we just need to get the application complete, so let's begin with the legal spelling of your first and last name."
- "To get this started, we just need an initial here."

Do you notice something about every statement above? Every statement is assuming the sale.

Always—and I mean always—assume the sale!

When you get to the end of the conversation, you never should say things like, "What do you think?" or "Does that price sound good?" or "Do you have any questions for me?" Remove all of these from your vocabulary—immediately! Your prospect had ample time during the earlier phases of the conversation to ask questions, to raise concerns, to express their hesitations. And, to be clear, with the Quote 3 conversation, you welcomed those questions and concerns. It wasn't as if you rushed through some sales agenda, trying to pull the wool over their eyes for a quick sale. You invited them to engage in a real dialogue with you. You listened actively and intently to their pain points and problems that they needed solved. You gave them ample time to ask questions and for you to provide more context and explanation as to why your product or service would help them. That's the beauty of the Quote 3 conversation. It is a real conversation, where you actually learn about your prospect and what they really need, and they learn from you how you can really help address those needs. So by the time you get to the close, you should feel good about where you are at with your prospect, and so you need to simply close the deal—and that starts by assuming the deal is done, assuming the sale.

When you deliver the price for your product or service, you need to assume the sale and go straight into what you need from them to get this processed so you can begin helping them. The time for letting them think and respond is over. If your product/service solves their problem, you've helped customers just like them, and you are the best fit for them, then they would be crazy not to do business with you today. They have a problem that needs fixed, and you have the solution. Solve it. Right then, in that moment.

Let's face it, you don't actually help the prospect until you turn them into a paying customer. You don't help them unless they actually buy from you. If they don't buy from you, they still have a problem that needs to be fixed.

Now, from being in sales myself for the last fifteen years and coaching and working with thousands of sales professionals, I know there is a real likely chance you are going to get nervous asking for money, especially if you are newer to sales. I know I was when I first started in sales. I know that just thinking about assuming the sale and asking for payment information makes you a little sick to your stomach and think, "I don't want to be pushy."

But let me reassure you: If you do everything we have talked about in this chapter, you will not come across as "pushy" or "sleazy" or any of the other words you fear being called. These are all fears that we think will happen, but that simply isn't true. It is a fake story you are making up in your head. It's just a fear you have to push through. The only way to overcome this fear and grow your confidence is to take action and do it! As with anything else in life, the more you do something the easier it is to do. The more you do something, the less scary it is. Think about the first time you drove a car, rode a bike, drank a beer, went on a date—first are always chock full of anxiety. The second time, less so. The third, even less. And, after a while, you don't think about it at all. It will just be like riding a bike.

Here is the fact of the matter in terms of your career. If you don't ask for payment information and if you don't go for the close, you are going to struggle to help customers and you are going to struggle to make money. You are going to struggle in sales. Asking for payment information is your job, duty, and obligation. If you don't help them, someone else is going to!

You can educate a customer until you're blue in the face, and you can share stories all you want. Those are crucial, vital, core aspects of sales. But don't be confused: *You cannot and will not help a prospect until they become a paying customer and buy your product/ service.* Period. End. This is the only way you solve their problem and help them. Once you truly understand, realize, and actually believe this, you will never have an issue asking for payment information ever again.

So again, think "Show me the money," always *assume* the sale, and finally always ask for payment information or whatever information you need to finalize the deal.

To close this all out, I want to share how Kat ended up. Prior to her implementing the Quote 3 method, Kat was an average producer at best, and I hope we can all agree, being average sucks! Kat wanted to get better!

So, she took action. She began practicing and roleplaying this conversation daily with her teammates and her spouse. She then began making sure she was having this conversation three times a day, every day. She had clarity in what it took daily, what the conversation needed to be, and what it looked like. By doing this, she saw immediate success. She instantly felt better about what she did for a living. She felt, in short, more fulfilled, happier, and more energized to embrace every day. Why? Because she felt like she was actually changing people's lives.

Within twelve months of incorporating the Quote 3 strategy, Kat went from barely making $50,000 a year to making over $100,000. In less than a year, she had doubled her income and was loving what she was doing. She was thriving, making a six-figure income and she was making a difference.

The distance between average and thriving isn't a huge gap and doesn't even typically require huge changes. To go from struggle to success is done by taking small, action steps every day! Kat was willing to try something new. Now it's your time to do the same.

7

PROOF IS IN THE PEOPLE! TIME TO GET MORE REFERRALS!

OLMAN SAYS VERY QUIETLY to me, "Stop and look at the Quetzal, the rarest bird in Costa Rica. This is your lucky day." We were standing on a swinging bridge in a cloud forest in Costa Rica early one morning.

I looked up, and there it was. The Quetzal was magical and beautiful. It is iridescent, which means, to the eye, it changes colors depending on its surroundings. If it is in the canopy of the tree tops, it appears green. When its feathers are illuminated by the sun, it appears gold. Talk about an amazing experience! But this was just one standout moment we had while working with Olman in Costa Rica.

Olman was our personal guide while visiting the cloud forest region of Costa Rica. He took us zip lining, bird watching, on a night walk through the forest to see all of the creatures that wake up and come out at night, a waterfall hike, and horseback riding. This was all over a three-day period. Not only did Olman do his "job" as a guide, taking us from one destination to another, he also talked about the history of Costa Rica, gave us the best recommendations for food and restaurants, and asked us a lot of questions about ourselves so he could get to know us better, so much so that by the end of day three, Olman didn't feel like a guide, he felt like a friend.

When the end of day three came, he dropped us off at the resort where we were staying. As we were saying our goodbyes, Olman said, "It's been a pleasure working with you all this week and getting to know you. Would you be willing to help me out by leaving a review on Yelp?"

"Absolutely!" we said.

Olman then proceeded to text us the Yelp link to make it easy on us. As he was texting over the link he said, "Thank you so much, this will really help me out. Out of curiosity, do you all know of anyone that plans to visit Costa Rica in the near future?"

Funny he asked, as it just so happened that our really great friends were headed to Costa Rica in seven weeks. We replied, "Actually, yes, we do. Our friends will be here in a couple of months."

Olman then said, "I would love to help your friends anyway I can. Would you be willing to connect us via the WhatsApp and I can help them with recommendations?"

And boom! Just like that, Olman asked for a referral. Not only did he ask for one, he got a *hot* one! Olman not only went above and beyond for us by providing exceptional customer service and an amazing experience, but he asked for a referral.

Olman wasn't the only guide we had while visiting Costa Rica. We had multiple guides, and honestly, they were all great. It was truly a great experience the entire time we were there (except our Ayahuasca experience, but that's a different story for a different day.) The one key difference between Olman and the other guides is that Olman was the *only* one who asked for a referral. Many asked for reviews, but that was it.

Guess what? Olman was the only one that *received* a referral!

Which leads me into this chapter. You want referrals, I want referrals, everyone wants referrals. Referrals are the best business by far. They are typically easier to talk to. Closing ratios tend to be double, sometimes triple compared to cold leads. They are coming from an ideal customer, so they typically tend to be an ideal customer as well. They also tend to do business with you for longer and repeatedly. Oh and referrals are *free*!

I would assume you agree with me that referrals are not only incredibly valuable but also essential for a thriving business. (You better be shaking your head yes.) I would also assume you are like every sales professional I work with, and you want *more* referrals. However, if you are like 95 percent of the sales professionals I work with, you can't remember the last time you asked for or got a referral. Let's put it to the test:

- Do you remember the last referral you got?
- Do you remember the last time you asked for a referral?

No shame here. I get it, it is easy to *not* ask. However let's go ahead an address the big fat elephant in the room. The two reasons you aren't getting referrals at all or not consistently is because:

1. You're not referable.
2. You don't ask for referrals.

Let's dive into these.

You're Not Referable: Myth or Reality?

Just be honest with yourself. You're not referable.

How does that feel? You may be agreeing with me right now or you may totally disagree with me. You may be triggered a little bit, which is totally normal and okay. Maybe even good because it shows you care. It shows you think more highly of yourself—and you should! You're a great person, and you do things for the right reasons. But—and this is a big *but*—are you providing a remarkable, transformational experience for your customer that makes them say, "Wow"? Are you just doing what they call "walk in and ask for" and then move on about your day?

It's important to ask these kinds of self-reflective, introspective questions about yourself—not just now but periodically. Why? Because we all get into ruts, we all can get complacent. We all might start to run on 80 percent rather than 100 percent. So asking yourself hard questions will keep you on your toes. And your toes are what you absolutely need to be on right now. So ask yourself a few more questions:

- Are you providing a transactional experience or a transformational one?
- When your customer gets off the phone with you, how do they typically feel?
- Are you going above and beyond or are you just doing your "job"?

I really want you to think about and reflect on these questions because it all leads to the ultimate question: Are you actually referable?

I personally believe that you are referable. How do I know this? How do I know this without even having met you? I know you're referable because you bought this book. Not only that, you're reading it. You're more than half-way through it. And why? Because you know you can do better, and, most importantly, you 100 percent *want* to do better. You're actively, in this very moment, trying to better yourself—for your business, for your customers, for your family, for yourself. A person with those kinds of values and passion is always referable. You just have to make sure you are executing in ways that lets people see it, day in and day out.

I believe that you are a lot like me early on in my career where I was just trying to get one customer sold and move on to the next. I believe that you are a lot like I was and merely looking at the on-going service transactions with current customers as just that, transactions that you have to do, get through, and complete so you can get back to prospecting and selling. You see, it's not that you aren't referable, you just aren't creating a referable experience. You're too worried about your next sale and hitting your production goals so you have a job next month.

To be referable and get more referrals requires a mindset shift. Not only is the initial experience critical as it sets the tone for the relationship moving forward, but every single interaction with that customer counts moving forward as well. It can't just be a party the first time and a funeral every time after. What paying customer wants that? Your first interaction must be transformational, and so should your second, and your third, and your fourth…. The party should never end!

The Quote 3 conversation makes sure that the experience is transformational from the beginning and sets you up for success to get referrals after that! But you have to make sure you bring that same energy and enthusiasm every time. I want you to think of a first date with a person you really like and really want to go on a second date with. You are, of course, going to make sure you bring your A-game to impress this person so much that they have no choice but to go out on a second date with you. It's the same concept with a client. Every interaction you have with them, you need to impress them so they want to keep doing business with you and telling their friends and family that they should also be doing business with you.

Here's a quick checklist for the right approach to making every interaction with your customers a transformational one:

- Slow down
- Be intentional with the person you are working with at the time, every time
- Give them your full attention
- Answer and solve their questions and problems

In more simplistic terms and truly as simple as I can make it, actually *care* about the person you are talking to and working with. Don't view them as just another task or box you have to check off for the day.

Now that you are referable, it's time to ask for referrals!

Ask for the Referral

Yes, you have to ask for what you want. Providing an amazing experience isn't enough. You have to go one extra step and actually ask. Just like you have to ask for payment details to close the deal, you are going to have to ask for referrals.

Here is the thing, your customers want to help you as well; they just don't know how to help you. Think of it outside of business. Think of a time when a friend was annoyed with you because you didn't help them with something. You may have been confused as to why they were mad, and so you ask them what the deal is. When they say it's because you didn't help them, your first response is likely, "Because you didn't ask!" You didn't know! You're not a mind reader! This same scenario might totally play out in the reverse too, where you have gotten mad at a friend or loved one, but didn't let them know you wanted or needed their help.

We all do this sometimes. We don't let people know we need help, even when we do. Sometimes it's out of pride—we don't want to admit we need help—or sometimes we just don't think to ask, or sometimes we assume people will "just know." But people typically don't "just know." People are busy. We all have tons of obligations and things to do each day that clutter our mind, that keep us preoccupied. At the end of the day, it's a bit arrogant, actually, to assume that people are always thinking so much about us and our personal needs and that they'll just always know what we want or need at any given moment. Which is exactly why you certainly can't assume your customers will "just know" either. You have to *ask* for it!

So I am going to cover my favorite way to ask for a referral, and then I'll share some strategies on the best *time* to ask for referrals.

I have tried multiple methods of asking for referrals and what I am about to share with you is the same word track that has not only worked for me and my businesses, but thousands of sales professionals I have worked with.

First you ask for help. "Hey John, would you be willing to help me out?"

They typically always respond with "Yes" or "Of course."

Then I reply, "Great! It's actually simple and will help me out a lot. First, let me ask you an easy question. Who is the first person you think of that could benefit from working with me?" (Pause for two seconds.) "Who was the first person that just came to your mind, John?"

They typically respond with a name. "Well, Adam might."

"That's great, thank you, John! How do you know Adam?" You see this is where I dig in a little and get them talking about their friend or family member and their relationship.

After John responds with how he knows Adam, I respond with, "What is Adam's phone number so I can give him a quick shout?"

Once I have obtained the number, I like to go one step further and say, "John, thank you so much! Just so I don't catch Adam off guard, would you be willing to do a quick text introduction between me and Adam? My number is…"

Just like that, you asked for a referral. You now know *how* to ask for a referral, how to ask for help. If I had to guess, the reason you haven't been asking for referrals is because you didn't know how.

I hope your main takeaway from the script above is to ask for help! In fact, that's always how you should refer to it as—help, not referrals. People love helping people, so that's the word you should use!

Accounting for Objections, Hesitations, and Rejections

Yes, I realize I gave you a perfect script of a perfect customer that just went along with the ask. Yes, I completely understand that in practice, things don't always go so smoothly. You will hear objections like "I am not comfortable giving you so and so's number" or hesitations like "You know, I really can't think of anyone right now" or "Hey, if I think of anyone, I will send them your way." These types of lines go on for days.

And, yes, you will get told no. You will get outright rejected. This is expected. This is part of it. You're in the wrong business if you can't handle rejection.

However, you will also get told "Yes!" You are going to get more names and more numbers immediately when you implement this ask. You also have to remember that you are planting seeds. Just like a farmer has to plant seeds every year and wait months and months before they can harvest the crop, referrals tend to work the same way. The ask is sometimes like planting the seed! You ask for the referral, you plant the seed, and you wait. Then weeks or sometimes months later, it bears fruit.

Ultimately, you have to pursue and focus on what you can control—and that is the ask. Simply by implementing a consistent referral ask into your daily routine, you will begin to fill your prospect funnel with leads so that you then start to get consistent referrals and business with ideal customers.

Remember, it's not about more. It's about filling your prospect funnel so that you can have three conversations a day where you are proposing your product/service and asking for the sale. That's it! Asking for referrals is just another strategy to keep your prospect funnel full so you can set yourself up for success by having three conversations a day, every day, with new prospects who could be potential business for you!

Best Times and Opportunities for the Ask

Now let's discuss some opportunities that are great for asking for referrals. The very first one that comes to mind is right after the initial point of sale. You just had an amazing conversation. You discovered the customer's problem. You went through your entire proposal, you asked for the sale, and they said yes! At this moment, they are excited. They just gave you payment information. Now, before you end the meeting, you need to ask for help. You need to ask for a referral. Why wouldn't they want to send their friends, family members, or co-workers to also have the same transformational experience they just received? This is the *best* time to ask for help!

Another strategy is right when you get done servicing the customer. They call in with a question, to update payment information, or to schedule a time to come in because they have a few questions. It doesn't really matter why they are calling. The point is, they *are* calling, and you are helping them—you're fixing a problem they have. This presents an opportunity.

First and foremost, you must, of course, provide great customer service and solve the problem they are calling about. After you get done solving their issue and provide a great customer experience, you should then ask for a referral. I know it's easy to just solve the problem, thank the customer, and hang up the phone so you can get back to prospecting and selling. You know what is also easy and takes less than sixty seconds? Asking them for a referral! Asking for their help!

All it takes is being intentional with the ask. I know I am asking you to get uncomfortable. Anytime you change the way things have been done and you try something new, it will be uncomfortable. But as we said at the start of all this, you need to embrace change. You need to get over your fear of the unknown. The unknown is only the unknown until you know it. Then it transforms into a familiar space—and this space will end up earning you a lot more money. Take the leap.

To be sure, you don't have to do this on the fly. As always, practice gets us closer to perfect. So one way to help with being more confident and comfortable is to practice with your peers, manager, spouse, family, whoever will listen and is willing to— wait for it—help you! The reason you are hesitant to do it is the exact reason you need to do it. You need to get over yourself and get over feeling "self-conscious." Asking the people you know to role-play this out with you is a great way to, well, get over yourself. The more you practice out loud in front of people, the more familiar and normal it will all become—which means the easier it will be for you when it really matters. Even just asking friends and family for help is, in a way, additional practice for asking your clients for help. So do it! Practice first and then implement.

Ultimately, anytime you talk to a customer and provide them with a great experience, you need to be asking for a referral. Consistently ask for referrals and you will consistently get referrals. There is nothing magical about this process. The magic is merely being disciplined with asking every customer every time!

8

TIME BLOCKING:
THE SET UP FOR SUCCESS

IT WAS 2014, AND I was in my first year of business ownership. I was the janitor, sales manager, leader, CEO, head of marketing, lead sales producer, community liaison, toilet cleaner—the list just kept going and going. Courtney and I had a team of two by our sides. Their primary role was sales and that was what I wanted them focused on. We didn't have much money, as I said $5,000 to our names when we started the business, so our backs were against the wall. I wasn't afraid of hard work, and I knew I could wear multiple hats and work sixteen- to eighteen-hour days, six to seven days a week and be just fine.

That was exactly what I did. Not just for a month or two, but for the first eighteen months of our business, it was like that. The problem with this is I developed some really bad habits. One of the worst habits I created was zero organization within my day. I had no plan. No regimen each day. I had no system to prioritize what I needed to do. If a customer would call in, I took it. If I heard a teammate on the phone, I'd go coach them in the moment, meaning I would go give instant feedback on what they could have done better or differently. If a community event were happening, I'd run out the door. Oh and somehow, I had to get my prospecting done to grow my business. When did that happen? Whenever I could squeeze it in between the other five hundred things I was trying to get done. Essentially, everything I did was reactive.

Do you remember the game Whack-A-Mole? If you don't, it's a game where there are multiple holes, a mole will pop up out of the holes randomly, and you have to hit it on the head with a hammer. This is what my day felt like, every single day. I would put out one fire and ten more had started. It was absolute chaos. Just telling you this story makes me cringe. The sickest part of the entire deal, I kind of liked it and made it work. Always on the go, always something to do. Insane, right?

So I was extremely busy, and actually felt okay with what I was doing, but was I productive? I asked myself this one day.

I felt like I was always busy, always doing something which made me feel productive. The problem, though, is I would get to the end of my day and wasn't quite sure what I accomplished, if anything. My day was so scattered, so reactive, so full of chaos, that I couldn't even be sure that I did anything at all. Sure I was always doing *something*, but was I doing the things that moved the needle in my business?

Eventually, I started to burn out. That honeymoon elation started to wane, and I finally had to face the hard truth. I was working sixteen to eighteen hours a day, sacrificing time away from my wife and family, and I wasn't being proactive at all. I wasn't getting my sales training in. I wasn't reading. I wasn't getting my prospecting done consistently. Team meetings weren't getting done. There were even some days where I had a hot lead I was supposed to follow up with, but I was so "busy" that time would either get away from me or I would simply forget. Then I noticed my team started doing the same thing and making the same excuses. They were duplicating my behavior. Chaos had taken over! I was modeling losing—not winning—behavior and practices!

As I said, this wasn't an overnight type of transition or behavior. It took me eighteen months to realize what was going on, and we were way past the stage of no return. I was experiencing burnout. My team was turning over frequently and was also experiencing burnout. Most of them weren't hitting their goals. I was questioning whether this was even for me anymore.

After a long conversation with Courtney, we determined that I did enjoy what I was doing, but I needed some serious structure. Not only did I need structure, my team needed structure and our business needed structure. It was time for a change!

So I started to research time management and ask other successful professionals how they managed their days. This is when my life and career changed for the better in a significant way! The trick? Time blocking!

Now, what is a time block? A time block is a designated time on the calendar for a specific activity you need to accomplish. For example, every morning from 8:30 a.m.. to 8:45 a.m. we have a team sales training meeting. Then from 8:45 a.m. to 9:00 a.m. we have our first team huddle (production meeting) of the day. These are blocks of time that are dedicated always and exclusively to these activities. Nothing else can or will happen during these time blocks.

Another example would be my meeting with my executive assistant time block. Every day, I have a quick fifteen-minute meeting with my EA from 9:30 a.m. to 9:45 a.m.. Again, this meeting at this time takes precedence over everything else. Nothing else will happen during this time for me and my EA except to meet for this block of time and go over the day's agenda. At this point, I swear by time blocks so much I even time block my eating schedule! If I don't have "eat" on my calendar, I don't eat. Sounds terrible, I know, but it's true. What is on the calendar is what gets done! Period.

I'm sharing this with you because this is the recipe for your success as a sales professional; this is the recipe for organizing your days. It's the recipe for setting priorities and creating accountability. Not only will you be more intentional with what you are doing, this will lead you to being more productive and making sure you are running your day instead of your day running you. You are being proactive instead of reactive. You are simply prioritizing what is important and what you are going to get done!

Time blocking is the way to quit playing Whack-A-Mole. Make time for prospecting by time blocking. Make time to accomplish your three conversations a day with new prospects by time blocking. Make time for eating by time blocking. You can make time for essentially everything in your life through time blocking. The key is that you actually have to follow your time-block schedule. You create it, but then you need to let it govern your day. It won't work if you create this awesome time-block schedule and then ignore it or cheat on it all the time.

This goes back to the discipline we said you needed to build through your morning routine. If you notice now in hindsight, my morning routine was actually time blocked! But if I miss something on a given day (which will of course happen from time to time), that's it. That activity will not get done on that day. Why? Because to do X activity after its designated time-blocked slot means that I would need to de-prioritize something on my schedule that I had prioritized. That kind of shifting is reactive and leads to what you're trying to get away from in the first place—deciding willy-nilly what you think you need to get done at any given moment. So you have to have the discipline to stick with the schedule. It might've sounded sad when I said I don't eat sometimes if it's not in the schedule, but that's actually an example of how disciplined I am with this and how much I trust this process. As with everything I've been telling you, you have to fully commit!

If you are anything like me, not only will this strategy help you immediately be more productive, you are going to feel more fulfilled in what you are doing because every day you feel accomplished. You prioritize the needle movers in your day, and you accomplish them! Not only did this strategy help me, my team thrived when I taught this strategy to them. Production skyrocketed. Not only did production skyrocket, everyone's work load seemed to decrease. Working less, making more. Everyone was much happier in their roles, including myself. And I've been time blocking ever since. Morning routine, team meetings, client appointments, prospecting, coaching calls, writing this book, and, yes, even eating! You name it, it's on the calendar.

This time blocking strategy changed my career and life! Which is exactly why I wanted to write this chapter and share it with you. I have shared the Quote 3 concept, we have broken down strategies to attract your ideal customer, and I broke down the conversation and showed you how to get more referrals, but here is the thing, if you don't prioritize what we have discussed in this book, nothing is going to change. That's why time blocking is so important.

I know things come up. I know change can be hard. I know some days it's like the fires just don't stop. This is exactly why incorporating time blocking is so important. It's going to take discipline. It's going to take saying *no* to things so you can say *yes* to things. Success takes being intentional with what you're doing and showing up day after day focusing on the needle movers, prioritizing what is important, and being disciplined with the process.

If you're tired of feeling overwhelmed, playing Whack-A-Mole daily, and not feeling fulfilled in what you do, implement time blocking today, start prioritizing what is important, and make sure you get your three conversations done daily.

9

QUOTE 3 CREATES A COHESIVE TEAM

IMAGINE THE SALES MANAGER and sales team all being on the same page. That would be pretty magical, right? Everyone knows what the goals are. Everyone knows what they are expected to do. Everyone knows exactly how to hit expectations. Everyone understands what marketing is being done. Everyone has similar sales conversations, so the data is easy to track and coach to. Everyone has time blocks on their calendar and runs an organized and efficient day. You have a culture that is self-managing, and everyone is winning and having fun, while feeling fulfilled in their role and not getting burnt out. This is a sales organization's dream! This is every company's dream. This is exactly what Quote 3 does for an organization and why Quote 3 is so powerful from not only an individual performance perspective, but also a team perspective. Quote 3 builds strong, sustainable, cohesive, and (most importantly) winning teams!

First, let's discuss clarity and accountability. I perform better when I know exactly what I am supposed to do. You perform better when you know exactly what you are supposed to do. Clarity is magical because clarity provides confidence and accountability. When you as the sales producer know exactly what is expected of you and how to accomplish those expectations, that is going to give you confidence to not only achieve, but exceed those expectations.

While clarity gives the sales producer confidence, it gives the sales manager confidence *and* the ability to know exactly what to track and hold the team accountable to. Instead of the sales manager just preaching to do *more*, now it's, "What ideas do you have to accomplish your three quotes today?" We are now tracking what's most important and holding the team accountable to what actually matters—conversations, as we discussed earlier. Maybe the motto in the organization is, "Just Quote 3!" Pretty simple to understand and get behind, right? And simplicity is key here. Life is complicated. People are complicated. That is why to be successful in sales, we want to keep it as simple and straightforward as possible.

The Quote 3 method eliminates any confusion there might be amongst the sales team and individuals. It also has the team hyper-focused on what matters. Not more calls, just three conversations a day, every day, where each team member is building rapport, discovering problems, proposing the product or service, and asking for the sale. That's it!

Quote 3 also allows the sales manager to be a better coach. For example, if someone isn't hitting their three quotes a day, it's going to be easy to understand why and nail down where the problem truly lies. Something might be wrong with the elevator pitch or maybe the prospecting isn't getting done. As we troubleshoot such a scenario, let's say we first see what prospecting is getting done and make sure there aren't hurdles getting in the way of the prospecting time blocks. Once that has been checked and discussed, maybe they are having a hard time overcoming the initial upfront objections in the Quote 3 conversation and just can't get past those hurdles. You can then start practicing that part of the conversation with your sale team member. Because we've removed all the clutter of *more* from our sales approach, it will be much easier to diagnose and resolve any problems like this.

Another example: Maybe your team is getting the three quotes done a day, but they aren't closing any of them. You can walk through the components of the Quote 3 conversation to see where the problem lies. You can listen to a recording of the sales conversation or role-play to identify what's wrong or what is missing or what it is they are forgetting. Are they building enough rapport? Are they having a discovery conversation and figuring out what's most important to the customer and what problems they have that need solved? Are they having an educational, empowering conversation with the customer or just going through the motions? Are they asking for payment information after delivering the price and assuming the sale? Quote 3 simplifies everything from coaching to training to expectations. It gets everyone on the same page and working from the same basic approach. Everyone is speaking the same language, and so it makes problems and challenges so much easier to identify and resolve so that, at the end of the day, everyone, every day, is winning!

A Winning Team is a Fun Team

Let's talk about winning for just a moment more. Winning is fun. When a team is winning, a team is having fun. When a team is having fun, the culture is going to be addicting and attractive. When you have a culture that is fun and addicting, you are going to have lower turnover. Remember Charlie? As I told you earlier, prior to implementing the Quote 3 method in his agencies, he had lost twenty-two employees in the previous three years. After implementing Quote 3, he lost only three people in the following two years! When you create a fun environment and winning culture, everyone in the organization looks forward to coming to work, including you. Winning makes everyone happy to come to work!

You are also willing to endure "suck" for success when there is an element of fun. Take us for example. We are in Kansas City. We have the best team in the NFL, the Kansas City Chiefs. It is fun to be a Chiefs fan. Every single game we know we have the ability to win. I mean we have won three Super Bowls since 2020 (not to brag or anything). Chiefs fans, including myself, will literally go out in the middle of winter, sit in a cold-ass outdoor stadium where it is snowing and the wind is swirling, and it is so cold that the snot running out of your nose and down your face will freeze in your mustache. We endure all of this to cheer our team on because it's fun and we are happy—because we are winning! (Go Chiefs!)

Not only is having fun critical for the current team and organization, but also think about new hires that are considering joining your organization. If your organization is lame and feels like a funeral home, that isn't going to attract top talent. Top talent, A-players want to be around other A-players. They want to be part of a winning environment. Quote 3 retains the talent you have, and it makes new hiring much easier as well!

And what's the biggest pain when it comes to new hires? Yep, training. Getting them up and over that learning curve so that they are fully aligned and on board with what you do and how you do it. But with Quote 3, not only are you attracting top talent and A-players because of a winning culture and organization, but also you now have a culture and training plan that is built on consistency. You have a streamlined process that you plug your new hire into that helps them be successful from day one. You are able to promote organization, efficiency, and professionalism. You are able to teach the new hire, from day one, what is going to be expected out of them using the Quote 3 methodology. You will teach them what marketing efforts will look like to support sales growth and what needs to be done to accomplish the three quotes a day. They will learn a proven sales conversation based on building relationships, discovering problems, and selling like a true professional. They will also learn exactly what they can expect to produce by utilizing the Quote 3 method and how much money they will make by achieving those sales goals. Clarity and confidence, baby!

Money, Recognition, Time

When it comes to motivation and what you and I want and expect out of an opportunity and organization, it typically comes down to three things: money, time, and recognition. Let's break these down real fast to help you determine how you are motivated.

- *Money motivated.* When you are motivated by money, that means that you are typically hungry to make more money and are going to be most motivated by money incentives like weekly or monthly bonuses. If you are money motivated, you are going to be looking for a very lucrative commission plan and opportunity as well. The better you get at your craft, the more sales you make, the more money you make.

- *Recognition motivated.* When you are motivated by recognition, you like your name in the spotlight. You like seeing your name at the top of the production report. You like earning trophies and trips. You like the shoutouts and you like that everyone else knows who you are and how good you are.

- *Time motivated.* When you are motivated by time, you value freedom and time off to yourself or to spend however you want. You want the ability to get the job done, crush the goals, and then enjoy your life outside of work. You like the ability to be incentivized with extra time off like additional vacation time or even being able to earn a Friday off a week or month.

Regardless of how you are motivated, the Quote 3 method allows you to thrive! Quote 3 is going to set you up for success to close a minimum of one new client every day, and even more as you master your craft and sales skills. This will ensure that you not only hit, but also exceed your goals, allowing you to make more money, be recognized as a top performer within your organization, and earn more time off. Depending on the industry you work in, for example, when you accomplish your three quotes for the day, you can enjoy the rest of the day off. This is exactly why Quote 3 is so powerful! You know exactly what to do every single day to make the money you want, be a top sales producer making multiple six and even seven figures, be recognized as the best in the company, and, all the while, have the time and freedom you want after you have accomplished your goals for the day.

The best part about this is you know exactly what is expected of you and how to win. You are having meaningful conversations every day that are going to keep you fulfilled in your career because you are truly making a difference in your customers' lives and not just pushing products to make a paycheck. You are also being rewarded the way you want, which keeps you motivated and looking forward to coming in to perform every day.

Customer Experience

Now let's talk just a little about the flip side of all this: the customer experience. When you are having fun, you are automatically going to come across confidently on the phone or in meetings. This is going to help your closing ratio be instantly better. Customers are not just going to hear the difference, they are going to feel the difference. The Quote 3 method and conversation not only is going to help you win, but it is also going to make sure the customer wins. You are going to be having a conversation with the customer that no other sales person has ever had with them before. Most sales people are so focused on the *more* method that customers are treated like just another number. The customer is going to hear the difference, feel the difference, and know without a doubt that you are the person they want to work with. They going to want to work with you, and they are going to send their friends and family your way as well.

Quote 3 is going to help you win, help the organization win, and help the customer win. Quote 3 is going to ensure you escape the rat race of sales and of always just doing more to hit your goals. It is going to make sure you are focused on what matters every day. All you have to do is Quote 3!

CHAPTER
10

HAPPY, HEALTHY, WEALTHY

IN DECEMBER 2021, AFTER two delicious bottles of red wine, Courtney and I made a decision that would soon become both our family and company motto. We discussed how we could live a life that was based on being happy, healthy, and wealthy. The first thing we decided that night was that we wanted to go on an adventure. We needed some excitement in our life. Courtney asked me, "What would you think if we bought an RV and traveled the west coast for a couple of months?" I responded with, "Let's do it!"

Four months later, we loaded up our two dogs (Rocky and Lola) and cat (Phoenix), left Kansas City, and headed to San Diego in our forty-four-foot Class A Entegra Coach! You read that right, forty-four feet long! Over the next three and a half months, we covered Oklahoma, Texas, New Mexico, Arizona, California, the Oregon Coast, Nevada, Utah, and Colorado. It was by far the most exciting and fun adventure I have ever had in life. At thirty-four years old, I was crossing the country in a motorhome, living in places I loved, making memories that will last forever with the people I love, and making the most money I had ever made in my life.

Life is extremely short, and you should be focused on the things that make you happy, healthy, and wealthy! For example, Courtney and I love to travel. Together, we have been to over twenty-six countries since 2016. We have also been to over forty states in the US. We have visited three of the seven wonders of the world (The Great Wall, The Colosseum, and Machu Picchu). Traveling around the world and around the United States, seeing different cultures, and meeting new people is what lights our souls on fire. It is our happy place, you could say.

This is our family motto because it forces us to prioritize what's important. Our happiness and health. If these two things are being prioritized, wealth will come. As Courtney always says, "Money follows fun," and I couldn't agree with her more. When you are doing the things you love and enjoy, you are going to have fun. When you are healthy and feeling good all of the time, you are going to have fun. When you are making money, are healthy, and are doing the things you love in life, that equates to a pretty full life. I would consider you very wealthy just like I consider myself very wealthy.

Happy, fulfilled individuals take care of themselves from a health perspective. If you're not sick or stressed, you're well-positioned to be maximally productive and able to hit your big goals. Once you're both happy and healthy, you're definitely going to be wealthy—however you define that. It can be money, freedom, travel, or great relationships with your kids, spouse, and co-workers.

This is why I believe in the Quote 3 methodology so much. It also promotes these three core values of living a happy, healthy, and wealthy lifestyle. I live and promote this approach because I don't believe in a "work–life balance"; it's just *life*! Working and making money is a part of life. Doing things that you love and bring you joy are also a part of life.

The important thing here in being able to create such a life for yourself is that Quote 3 promotes healthy *boundaries* because it focuses on being intentional with what matters most in your sales career. Boundaries in life are vital, but they're not always easy to set, especially when it comes to work. When is enough *enough*? How many hours are enough? Do you make that extra call? Pay that extra visit? Send that extra text or email? The Quote 3 method sets all those boundaries for you, which helps reduce the stress and pressure of having to try to set and maintain these types of boundaries yourself. It also frees up your mental space to focus on what truly matters in your life—being happy, healthy, and wealthy. Get your three quotes done in a day, make a sale or two on the day, and go have fun. Quality conversations, quality relationships, quality career, and a quality life! It's that simple.

What I don't want to happen to you is that you put living your life on hold. You don't take the trip you want to because you'll "do it in retirement." You don't buy your dream house because you'll "do it in retirement." You don't have any hobbies because that is what retirement is for. But what if before you have the chance to retire, you have a heart attack and die because of all the stress you are under from all those things you promised yourself and your family you would do? What if you keep putting it off, and putting it off, and then it never happens? I am here to tell you that you can make the money you want to while also living your dream life that you want to have. That is exactly why the Quote 3 approach is so important and so powerful.

You got into sales to change people's lives. You got into sales to change your life. You got into sales to make a lot of money. But right now you find yourself unfulfilled, not making the money you want, and on the verge of burnout, and you're not having fun at all. You are being hit by the freight train of doing *more* head on. Now is the time for change before it's too late and the freight train hits you so hard that you can't recover from it. So let's focus on these three elements for just a few moments. Let's take some time to reflect on what being happy, healthy, and wealthy means to you.

I want you to start with happiness. What makes you happy? What brings you joy? What hobbies are you putting off doing that would bring you happiness? What else are you putting off that would bring you fulfillment? What are three things you want to accomplish and do between now and the next three years in life? What makes you happy and what do you enjoy in your career? How can Quote 3 help increase your overall happiness and fulfillment in your career?

Now I want you to think about your health. Just like I had you determine your new success routine in Chapter 2, now I want you to think about what else you can do to improve your health because health is key to everything, right? You need to optimize your health to optimize your productivity, which will allow you to accomplish what makes you happy and wealthy. So how is your new success routine going to improve your health? How often are you eating and what are you eating? What ideas do you have to improve your health even further? How would being healthier positively affect your life and career? How does Quote 3 help you accomplish your health goal?

And last but not least, wealth! The most important question is what does wealth mean to you? How much money do you have in savings? How much money do you have in investments? How much money are you making? How much do you work? What do your days look like? How much time do you spend with your family? What are you doing on vacations? What is it that you absolutely love and want to do more of? Are you working remotely or in the office? How does Quote 3 help you accomplish your wealth goals?

If you are anything like me, if things aren't going well at work, things aren't going well at home, and vice versa—if things aren't going well at home, things aren't going to go well at work. Adopting the Quote 3 method will help make sure that your career is going well so that your life can go well!

11

TAKE ACTION!

YOU NOW KNOW WHAT it takes to crush it as a sales professional. You have heard Charlie's story, Kat's story, and even Olman's story. The one thing they all had in common: Action. They were willing to get out of their comfort zone, whether that was asking for referrals, being willing to learn something new, or being willing to change. They all took action to advance themselves closer to their goals, who they wanted to be, and how they wanted to live. You have to do the same. Yes, you took action reading this book, but it can't stop there. You need to keep going. You now need to implement and apply what you've learned on a daily basis to affect positive change in your life. You need, quite simply, to take action!

To be successful in sales—and I mean to be really successful in sales, crushing it successful—it's not all that difficult. Just follow all that we discussed and learned about in this book.

First, you must be disciplined. Disciplined to a daily routine where you are working on your physical, mental, emotional, and spiritual health. Disciplined to self-development and growth which I already know you are doing because you are reading this book. Disciplined to narrowing down and being very specific with who your ideal customer is and speaking to that ideal customer. Disciplined to marketing and prospecting daily and filling your pipeline so that you can always talk to three new customers a day, every single day. Disciplined to then ask for a referral when you help a customer. Disciplined to take it one day at a time and focus on what needs to be done that given day to accomplish the Quote 3 method.

I know days can be tough. I know days can go sideways. I know that sales can be difficult. But sales is the greatest opportunity in the world. You have the ability to help people every day, make a difference in people's lives, and make a lot of money in the process so you can live the life of your dreams while also loving what you do for a living. The best part is it just comes down to three conversations a day, every single day. That's it! Three conversations a day are what allow you to make the money you want and live the life you want.

Are you committed to taking control of your life? Are you committed to not going extinct and being replaced by technology? Are you committed to making the money you want and deserve? Are you committed to success and crushing it as a sales professional? Are you committed to living a happy, healthy, and wealthy life? Commitment starts with taking action. Get your daily routine on the calendar, block out time for prospecting, and block out time for your three conversations daily. Take control of your day and control of your life and future!

You are the only person in charge of your future success, no one else. Go out and take control of your future! Take action!

ABOUT THE AUTHOR

MICHAEL WEAVER IS AN author, speaker, host of the top rated insurance podcast, *The Insurance Buzz*. He is also the founder of Weaver Sales Academy, a sales training organization for insurance professionals who are responsible for over $200 million in sales. Michael has over two decades of experience owning and operating sales organizations and has coached over 10,000 sales professionals globally.

When he's not working, Michael and his wife, Courtney, are avid travelers and adventurers and like to spend as much time outside as possible. When they aren't living on the edge, you can find them at their Midwest lake house with their two dogs, Rocky and Lola, and one-eyed cat, Phoenix, spending time with family and friends.